QoS in IP Networks: Prioritization, Classification, and Traffic Shaping

James Relington

DEDICATION

To those who seek knowledge, inspiration, and new perspectives—
may this book be a companion on your journey, a spark for curiosity,
and a reminder that every page turned is a step toward discovery.

AKNOWLEDGEMENTS

I would like to express my deepest gratitude to everyone who contributed to the creation of this book. To my colleagues and mentors, your insights and expertise have been invaluable. A special thank you to my family and friends for their unwavering support and encouragement throughout this journey.

Chapter 1: Introduction to Quality of Service

Quality of Service, commonly abbreviated as QoS, is a fundamental concept in the field of computer networking, especially within IP-based networks. At its core, QoS refers to the set of techniques and mechanisms used to manage network resources by prioritizing certain types of traffic, ensuring reliable delivery, and maintaining the performance of critical applications. As networks have evolved from simple data transmission systems into complex, multi-service infrastructures supporting voice, video, cloud computing, and interactive applications, the demand for intelligent traffic management has become more pressing than ever. This increasing dependency on high-performance networking has propelled QoS into the spotlight as a crucial component in maintaining efficiency, consistency, and user satisfaction.

The Internet was originally designed around the principle of best-effort delivery. This means that all data packets are treated equally, regardless of their content or origin, and are forwarded through the network with no guarantees regarding latency, jitter, or packet loss. While this approach was sufficient in the early days of the Internet when traffic was mostly limited to email and file transfers, it quickly became a limitation as real-time applications such as Voice over IP (VoIP), online gaming, and video conferencing became commonplace.

These applications are sensitive to delay and interruptions, and their performance can degrade significantly in congested or poorly managed networks. Therefore, the need to distinguish and treat traffic differently based on its nature and requirements gave rise to the development and implementation of QoS mechanisms.

QoS is fundamentally about providing differentiated treatment to different types of network traffic. Some applications require high bandwidth, others need low latency, and some are particularly sensitive to packet loss or jitter. For instance, streaming a video may tolerate a few dropped packets but requires a steady stream of data to avoid buffering. On the other hand, a voice call needs low latency and minimal jitter to ensure natural communication. In contrast, file downloads and software updates are generally not time-sensitive and can be delayed or throttled with minimal impact on user experience. By analyzing these needs, QoS enables networks to deliver more predictable and efficient service to each type of traffic.

One of the most important aspects of QoS is classification. Classification involves identifying and grouping packets based on attributes such as application type, source or destination IP address, port numbers, or even more advanced criteria such as application-level information. Once traffic is classified, it can be assigned different levels of service. For example, real-time voice traffic may be given high priority and low delay handling, while large file transfers might be relegated to a lower priority queue to avoid interfering with more urgent communications. This type of traffic differentiation is essential in ensuring that critical applications perform optimally even under heavy network load.

Another core component of QoS is traffic shaping and policing. These techniques involve controlling the flow of traffic entering or exiting a network in order to conform to specified performance parameters. Shaping smooths traffic flows by delaying packets when necessary to avoid sudden bursts that could overwhelm the network. Policing, on the other hand, enforces traffic limits by dropping or remarking packets that exceed predefined thresholds. Both methods are vital in maintaining network stability and fairness, particularly in shared environments where multiple users or applications are competing for limited bandwidth.

The implementation of QoS can take place at various layers of the network and can involve both hardware and software components. At Layer 2, technologies like IEEE 802.1p allow for basic traffic prioritization, while at Layer 3, the Differentiated Services Code Point (DSCP) field in the IP header provides a more sophisticated mechanism for marking and identifying different service classes. These markings allow routers and switches throughout the network to make forwarding and scheduling decisions that align with the intended QoS policies. The network devices may implement techniques such as queuing, prioritization, and resource reservation to ensure that each class of traffic receives appropriate treatment.

As networks scale and diversify, managing QoS becomes more complex. Enterprises and service providers must account for a wide range of variables, including the number of users, the diversity of applications, fluctuating traffic patterns, and potential points of congestion. They must also balance the competing needs of different stakeholders, ensuring that critical business operations receive the necessary support without entirely starving less important services. This challenge requires not only robust technical solutions but also clear policy frameworks and consistent monitoring and enforcement mechanisms.

QoS is not only about ensuring high performance; it is also a strategic tool for optimizing resource utilization and reducing operational costs. By enabling intelligent traffic management, organizations can make better use of existing infrastructure, delay costly upgrades, and improve the user experience without overprovisioning bandwidth. Furthermore, in environments where service-level agreements (SLAs) are in place, such as with Internet service providers or managed service platforms, QoS becomes essential in meeting contractual obligations and maintaining customer trust.

Another key benefit of QoS is its ability to support convergence. As networks increasingly carry multiple types of traffic over the same infrastructure—data, voice, video, and control signals—QoS ensures that each type of traffic is handled appropriately, reducing the risk of interference and ensuring smooth operation. This convergence enables more flexible and cost-effective architectures but would be impossible to achieve reliably without the granularity and control provided by QoS techniques.

QoS also plays a critical role in the adoption of emerging technologies. As organizations embrace cloud computing, edge computing, the Internet of Things (IoT), and 5G, the demand for consistent and adaptive QoS mechanisms continues to grow. These technologies introduce new challenges in terms of latency, bandwidth, and dynamic traffic flows, further underscoring the importance of QoS as a foundation for future-proof network design.

Ultimately, Quality of Service is not a one-size-fits-all solution but rather a dynamic set of tools and practices that must be tailored to the specific needs of each network. Whether implemented in a small enterprise network or a global service provider backbone, QoS remains one of the most critical components in ensuring that networks are not only functional but also efficient, reliable, and capable of meeting the evolving demands of the digital world.

Chapter 2: Historical Evolution of QoS in IP Networks

The concept of Quality of Service (QoS) in IP networks has undergone a significant transformation since the early days of computer networking. Understanding its historical evolution provides valuable insight into why QoS is so critical today and how it has adapted to the changing demands of applications, users, and network technologies. When IP networking was first developed, the primary focus was on connectivity and reachability. The Internet Protocol was designed to be a simple, scalable method of delivering data packets from one point to another, with very few guarantees about the timing or order of delivery. The best-effort delivery model of IP was considered sufficient at the time, as most early applications, such as email, file transfers, and simple web browsing, were not sensitive to delay, jitter, or loss.

In the 1970s and early 1980s, networks were relatively small and homogeneous. The ARPANET, the precursor to the modern Internet, demonstrated the feasibility of packet-switched networking, but it did not prioritize or differentiate between different types of traffic. The emphasis was on ensuring data delivery across disparate systems and architectures, and the network's limited use cases did not demand fine-grained control over traffic flows. However, as networks grew in scale and began supporting more varied applications, the limitations of the best-effort model became apparent. Particularly with the advent of voice and video over IP, the need for mechanisms to provide predictable and reliable service became increasingly urgent.

The first real steps toward QoS began in the late 1980s and early 1990s. During this period, research into real-time networking and multimedia communication gained momentum. The Internet Engineering Task Force (IETF) began to explore frameworks that could provide better service differentiation. This led to the introduction of the Integrated Services (IntServ) model. IntServ was designed to provide end-to-end QoS guarantees by reserving resources along the path of a data flow. It used the Resource Reservation Protocol (RSVP) to signal these reservations to each router in the path. IntServ aimed to deliver guaranteed bandwidth, bounded delay, and minimal jitter for applications like video conferencing and real-time voice.

While the goals of IntServ were ambitious and theoretically sound, its practical implementation faced serious scalability challenges. The stateful nature of IntServ required each router in the network to maintain detailed information about every flow passing through it. This was manageable in small networks but became untenable in large-scale, high-speed environments with millions of concurrent flows. As a result, while IntServ remained useful for certain controlled or limited applications, it did not become the dominant model for QoS in the broader Internet.

In response to the limitations of IntServ, the IETF proposed the Differentiated Services (DiffServ) model in the late 1990s. DiffServ marked a significant shift in QoS philosophy. Rather than trying to guarantee resources for individual flows, DiffServ introduced a simpler and more scalable approach by classifying and marking packets at the edge of the network. These packets were then treated according to predefined behavior classes as they traversed the core of the network. The key advantage of DiffServ was its ability to scale, thanks to its stateless operation in the core and its reliance on traffic aggregation rather than individual flow tracking. DiffServ used the DSCP (Differentiated Services Code Point) field in the IP header to indicate the desired service level, enabling routers and switches to prioritize traffic accordingly.

As DiffServ gained traction, network equipment vendors began integrating QoS capabilities into their devices. Routers and switches became more sophisticated, supporting a variety of queuing, scheduling, and policing mechanisms that allowed network administrators to implement complex traffic management policies. The early 2000s saw the widespread deployment of QoS in enterprise and service provider networks, particularly in environments that supported voice over IP (VoIP) and video conferencing. These technologies placed strict requirements on network performance, and QoS played a critical role in ensuring call quality and service continuity.

During this time, the rise of MPLS (Multiprotocol Label Switching) also contributed to the evolution of QoS. MPLS offered a way to route traffic based on labels rather than IP addresses, allowing for more efficient and predictable forwarding. It also supported traffic engineering and class-of-service mechanisms that enhanced QoS capabilities across wide-area networks. MPLS became particularly popular among service providers offering virtual private networks (VPNs) and managed services to enterprise customers, enabling them to provide differentiated service levels and meet service-level agreements (SLAs).

As the Internet continued to evolve, the nature of traffic changed dramatically. The emergence of video streaming, online gaming, cloud computing, and mobile applications introduced new challenges for QoS. These applications demanded not only low latency and jitter but also high throughput and reliability. At the same time, the decentralization of content through content delivery networks (CDNs) and edge computing architectures shifted the traffic patterns within networks, requiring QoS mechanisms to adapt to more dynamic and distributed environments.

More recently, the advent of software-defined networking (SDN) and network function virtualization (NFV) has further transformed the

QoS landscape. These technologies decouple the control and data planes, enabling more centralized and programmable traffic management. SDN, in particular, allows for real-time QoS policy adjustments based on application requirements, user behavior, or network conditions. This level of flexibility was difficult to achieve with traditional network architectures and represents a significant step forward in the evolution of QoS.

At the same time, the rollout of 5G networks and the proliferation of IoT devices are introducing new dimensions to QoS. 5G is designed with native support for network slicing, a concept that allows operators to create virtual networks with specific QoS characteristics tailored to different use cases. This includes ultra-reliable low-latency communications (URLLC), massive machine-type communications (mMTC), and enhanced mobile broadband (eMBB), each with unique performance requirements. Similarly, IoT networks often involve large numbers of devices with limited bandwidth and power, necessitating lightweight and efficient QoS mechanisms.

The historical journey of QoS in IP networks reflects the ongoing struggle to balance performance, scalability, and complexity. From its roots in best-effort delivery to the sophisticated, policy-driven models of today, QoS has evolved in response to technological advances and changing user demands. As networks continue to expand and diversify, QoS will remain an essential tool for ensuring that the digital experience meets the expectations of both consumers and enterprises across the globe.

Chapter 3: Fundamentals of IP Networking

Understanding the fundamentals of IP networking is essential for grasping how modern digital communication systems function and for appreciating the context in which Quality of Service mechanisms operate. Internet Protocol, or IP, lies at the core of network communication, serving as the principal mechanism for delivering packets of data across diverse and interconnected networks. It is a protocol that governs how information is formatted, addressed, transmitted, routed, and received on a network. IP is part of the larger

TCP/IP suite, a foundational model for network communication developed in the 1970s and still widely used today.

At its essence, IP networking operates on a packet-switching paradigm. In contrast to circuit-switched networks, where a dedicated path is established for the entire duration of a communication session, packet-switched networks divide data into smaller units known as packets. Each packet travels independently through the network and may take different paths to reach the destination. Once all packets arrive, they are reassembled into the original message. This approach allows for more efficient utilization of network resources and enables scalability across large and heterogeneous infrastructures.

An IP packet consists of two main parts: the header and the payload. The header contains crucial information used for routing and delivery, such as the source and destination IP addresses, the packet's length, fragmentation flags, and a time-to-live (TTL) field that prevents packets from circulating indefinitely. The payload carries the actual data being transmitted, whether that be a web page, an email, a voice sample, or any other form of digital content. The header also includes fields that allow higher-layer protocols like TCP, UDP, or ICMP to function effectively and communicate their needs to the network.

There are two versions of IP currently in use: IPv4 and IPv6. IPv4, the fourth version of the Internet Protocol, has been the dominant version since its creation. It uses 32-bit addresses, allowing for approximately 4.3 billion unique IP addresses. As the Internet expanded, it became clear that IPv4's address space would eventually be exhausted. This led to the development of IPv6, which uses 128-bit addresses, enabling a virtually limitless number of devices to be uniquely identified on the network. IPv6 also brings other improvements, such as simplified packet headers, better support for mobile devices, and enhanced security features. Nevertheless, IPv4 remains widely deployed, and the transition to IPv6 is still ongoing in many parts of the world.

Routing is a fundamental aspect of IP networking. Routers are specialized devices that examine the destination IP address of incoming packets and determine the optimal path for those packets to take through the network. They use routing tables, which contain information about network topology, to make these decisions. Routing can be either static, where routes are manually configured and do not change, or dynamic, where routers use protocols such as OSPF, BGP, or EIGRP to exchange information and adapt to changing network conditions. Dynamic routing enhances fault tolerance and optimizes network performance by allowing routes to be updated automatically in response to congestion or link failures.

Subnetting is another critical concept in IP networking. Subnets allow a larger network to be divided into smaller, more manageable segments. This improves routing efficiency, enhances security, and helps in organizing the network in a logical manner. Subnets are defined using subnet masks, which specify how many bits of the IP address are used for the network portion and how many are available for hosts. This hierarchical addressing scheme helps reduce the size of routing tables and facilitates better traffic management within large networks.

IP networking also involves the use of address translation techniques such as NAT, or Network Address Translation. NAT allows multiple devices on a private network to share a single public IP address when accessing the Internet. This conserves public IP addresses and provides a layer of security by masking internal IP addresses from external networks. Variants such as PAT (Port Address Translation) enable even more efficient sharing by mapping multiple internal IP addresses to different ports on a single external address.

Beyond routing and addressing, IP networking supports a range of auxiliary protocols and services that are essential for its operation. The Domain Name System, or DNS, translates human-readable domain names into IP addresses, enabling users to access websites and services without having to memorize numeric addresses. DHCP, or Dynamic Host Configuration Protocol, automatically assigns IP addresses to devices on a network, simplifying the configuration process and reducing administrative overhead. ICMP, the Internet Control Message Protocol, is used for diagnostics and error reporting, playing a key role in tools such as ping and traceroute.

Scalability, resilience, and interoperability are hallmarks of IP networking. It is designed to operate across any underlying physical medium, from copper wires and fiber optics to wireless radio signals.

This flexibility has enabled IP to become the universal language of the Internet, supporting a vast array of devices and applications. It also provides the foundation for more complex protocols and technologies, including QoS, virtual private networks (VPNs), mobile IP, and multicast communication.

Another vital characteristic of IP networking is its statelessness. IP does not maintain session information about the data packets it transmits. Each packet is treated independently and contains all the information necessary for its delivery. While this approach simplifies the design and increases scalability, it also places the burden of ensuring reliable communication on higher-layer protocols such as TCP. For applications that require more deterministic delivery, such as streaming media or VoIP, additional mechanisms such as QoS are required to provide the necessary performance guarantees.

As networks continue to expand in scale and complexity, the importance of understanding IP fundamentals becomes even more apparent. From homes and enterprises to global data centers and Internet backbones, IP networking underpins the connectivity that modern society depends on. Its foundational role is not only limited to traditional computing environments but extends to emerging technologies such as the Internet of Things, autonomous vehicles, and smart cities. Each of these relies on robust, scalable, and interoperable IP networking to function reliably and efficiently. The ongoing evolution of IP standards and practices ensures that it remains capable of supporting the growing demands of an increasingly connected world.

Chapter 4: The Need for QoS in Modern Networks

As digital communication has evolved, the demands placed on network infrastructure have grown significantly in both complexity and scale. Modern networks are no longer limited to simple data transfers between a few endpoints. Instead, they are expected to support a wide array of applications and services, many of which have strict performance requirements. From high-definition video streaming and real-time voice communication to mission-critical cloud applications and interactive gaming, today's network traffic is highly diverse. This diversity introduces challenges in ensuring that each application receives the level of service it requires. This is precisely where Quality of Service, or QoS, becomes essential in managing network performance and delivering consistent user experiences.

Modern networks must support a wide spectrum of services, each with unique characteristics and performance sensitivities. Voice over IP, for instance, is particularly sensitive to latency and jitter. Even minor delays can disrupt the flow of conversation and make communication difficult. Video conferencing and streaming services require consistent bandwidth and low packet loss to avoid visual artifacts and buffering interruptions. On the other hand, data-centric applications such as email, software updates, or cloud-based file storage are more tolerant of delay but can be bandwidth-intensive. In such a heterogeneous environment, treating all traffic equally under a best-effort model leads to unpredictable and often suboptimal performance, especially during periods of congestion.

The explosion of cloud computing has further intensified the need for QoS. Businesses increasingly rely on Software as a Service platforms, hosted virtual desktops, and remote collaboration tools. These applications are hosted offsite and accessed over the public internet or enterprise WANs, making network performance a key determinant of productivity. A single bottleneck in the path between user and application can degrade responsiveness, disrupt workflows, and impact business continuity. QoS mechanisms allow network administrators to prioritize critical business traffic over less urgent data, ensuring that vital services remain unaffected by congestion or high usage.

Another major driver of QoS adoption is the proliferation of mobile and wireless devices. With the rise of smartphones, tablets, and laptops, users expect uninterrupted connectivity and consistent application performance regardless of location. Wireless networks, especially Wi-Fi, are inherently more prone to congestion and interference than wired connections. Limited spectrum, variable signal strength, and competing devices in dense environments can significantly impact performance. QoS on wireless networks helps mitigate these issues by managing airtime, prioritizing latency-sensitive traffic, and ensuring fair access to shared resources. This is particularly important in environments like airports, conference centers, hospitals, and universities where large numbers of users are simultaneously connected.

The Internet of Things (IoT) introduces yet another layer of complexity to modern networks. IoT devices often generate small, periodic data packets but require high reliability and predictable delivery times. In industrial settings, IoT is used for automation, monitoring, and control systems that depend on real-time communication. Failing to prioritize this traffic could lead to delayed alerts, operational inefficiencies, or even safety hazards. QoS enables networks to distinguish IoT communications from bulk data transfers or streaming media, ensuring that time-sensitive messages are delivered promptly and reliably.

Service providers also depend on QoS to meet their operational goals and contractual obligations. Many offer tiered service plans that promise different levels of performance to consumers and businesses. These might include guarantees on bandwidth, latency, or uptime, often defined in Service Level Agreements. To honor these commitments, providers must implement QoS mechanisms that differentiate traffic, allocate resources accordingly, and monitor performance in real time. Without QoS, providers would be unable to offer these guarantees or maintain the quality required for premium services. Furthermore, they would struggle to manage peak usage periods, when the risk of congestion is highest and customer satisfaction is most at risk.

Security is another area where QoS plays a role. In the event of a denial-of-service attack or sudden traffic surge, QoS policies can be used to protect essential services from being overwhelmed. By enforcing rate limits, shaping traffic, or prioritizing trusted applications, networks can maintain operational stability even under adverse conditions. This kind of resilience is particularly valuable in sectors like finance, healthcare, and emergency response, where uninterrupted communication is vital and downtime can have serious consequences.

Video content now accounts for the majority of global internet traffic. Services like on-demand video streaming, live broadcasts, and video conferencing are integral to entertainment, education, and business. These services require not only high bandwidth but also sustained throughput and minimal buffering. The user experience is highly sensitive to variations in delivery quality. In educational settings, virtual classrooms rely on uninterrupted video streams to facilitate learning. In professional environments, video conferencing connects teams and clients around the world, making clear and consistent communication a top priority. QoS ensures that video traffic is prioritized when necessary, reducing buffering and enhancing the overall experience.

Interactive applications such as online gaming and remote desktop tools also place unique demands on network performance. These applications require low latency and minimal jitter to ensure responsiveness and a smooth user interface. In competitive gaming, milliseconds can make the difference between winning and losing. In technical support or remote administration, delays can lead to errors and frustration. By allocating higher priority to these interactive flows, QoS enables real-time feedback and control that would otherwise be degraded by background traffic.

With the growing adoption of virtualized and software-defined networks, QoS has also become more flexible and programmable. Network administrators can dynamically adjust policies based on changing conditions, user needs, or application behavior. For instance, during a large-scale video conference, the network can automatically allocate more resources to ensure optimal quality. Later, as the event ends and demand decreases, those resources can be reallocated to other services. This agility is critical in modern IT environments, where responsiveness and efficiency are key competitive advantages.

QoS is not merely a technical feature but a strategic enabler of digital transformation. It allows organizations to optimize the performance of their existing infrastructure, delay costly upgrades, and ensure that critical services receive the attention they deserve. By controlling how traffic flows across the network, QoS empowers administrators to deliver consistent, high-quality experiences to users, regardless of workload or traffic conditions. As networks become more complex and essential to daily life, the role of QoS in maintaining order, performance, and user satisfaction continues to grow in importance.

Chapter 5: QoS Models: Best Effort vs. Guaranteed Delivery

Quality of Service in IP networks is implemented through various models that determine how traffic is handled, prioritized, and delivered. Among these models, two fundamental approaches stand out as the most basic and widely understood: best effort and guaranteed delivery. These two models represent opposite ends of the QoS spectrum. Best effort is the simplest and most traditional model, while guaranteed delivery represents a more advanced and resource-intensive approach. Understanding the characteristics, strengths, and limitations of each model is crucial to designing networks that can support the wide range of applications and performance expectations found in modern environments.

The best effort model is the default mode of operation in IP-based networks. Under this model, all traffic is treated equally, without any differentiation or prioritization. Routers and switches forward packets as quickly as possible, depending on their current load and available resources. There is no guarantee that a packet will arrive on time, in the correct order, or even at all. This approach works well for applications that are tolerant to delay, packet loss, and variations in delivery time. Early Internet services like email, file transfers, and web browsing were primarily built with best effort delivery in mind. These applications can tolerate fluctuations in performance without significantly affecting the user experience.

Despite its simplicity, best effort delivery has significant limitations in today's complex networking environments. As more real-time and interactive applications emerged, the shortcomings of this model became evident. Voice and video communication, online gaming, virtual reality, and cloud-based services require consistent performance and low latency. Best effort networks are unable to ensure the level of reliability and responsiveness needed by such applications.

During periods of congestion, all packets compete equally for bandwidth, which often results in packet drops and increased delays for critical services. The lack of predictability can degrade the user experience and reduce the overall effectiveness of applications that rely on stable and timely communication.

In response to these challenges, the concept of guaranteed delivery was introduced. This model aims to provide a higher level of service by reserving or allocating network resources for specific traffic types. Guaranteed delivery involves mechanisms that ensure packets are delivered with minimal delay, low jitter, and negligible loss. This approach is particularly important for applications with stringent performance requirements, such as VoIP, video conferencing, financial transactions, and industrial automation. By providing assurances about network behavior, guaranteed delivery enhances reliability and enables the use of IP networks for mission-critical operations.

To implement guaranteed delivery, networks must incorporate sophisticated QoS mechanisms. One such mechanism is traffic classification, which identifies and categorizes packets based on predefined criteria, such as protocol type, application, source and destination addresses, or port numbers. Once traffic is classified, it can be marked for specific handling using fields in the packet headers, such as the Differentiated Services Code Point (DSCP) in IP headers. This marking allows routers and switches to apply appropriate queuing, scheduling, and policing policies.

Resource reservation is another key aspect of guaranteed delivery. In the Integrated Services (IntServ) model, the Resource Reservation Protocol (RSVP) is used to reserve bandwidth along the path from sender to receiver. Each router along the path commits to providing the requested level of service for the duration of the communication session. While this model provides precise control over resource allocation, it introduces overhead and complexity, as routers must maintain state information for every flow. This makes IntServ less scalable for large networks, particularly those with many simultaneous connections.

An alternative approach is the Differentiated Services (DiffServ) model, which offers a more scalable solution by aggregating flows into classes and providing per-class rather than per-flow QoS treatment. DiffServ does not guarantee specific delivery parameters for individual flows, but it does allow network administrators to assign higher priority and more bandwidth to certain classes of traffic. While not a true guaranteed delivery model in the strictest sense, DiffServ can approximate guaranteed service levels for critical applications when implemented correctly and consistently across the network.

The guaranteed delivery model also involves active management of network congestion. This includes techniques such as traffic shaping, which smooths traffic flows to prevent sudden bursts, and traffic policing, which enforces bandwidth limits and drops or marks packets that exceed predefined thresholds. These controls help maintain stability and ensure that high-priority traffic can pass through the network even during peak usage periods.

Although guaranteed delivery offers significant benefits, it also comes with challenges. Implementing it requires a deeper understanding of network behavior, precise configuration, and ongoing monitoring. It may also involve higher infrastructure costs, as network devices must support advanced QoS features, and additional bandwidth may be provisioned to accommodate reserved traffic. Furthermore, guaranteed delivery must be coordinated end-to-end, meaning all intermediate devices must honor the QoS markings and policies. In multi-vendor or cross-provider scenarios, this consistency can be difficult to achieve, potentially undermining the effectiveness of the model.

Many modern networks adopt a hybrid approach, combining elements of both best effort and guaranteed delivery. Routine, non-critical traffic is handled using the best effort model, while high-priority traffic is managed with QoS policies that approximate guaranteed delivery. This balance allows networks to remain efficient and cost-effective while meeting the needs of sensitive applications. It also aligns with the trend toward dynamic and adaptive networking, where QoS settings can be adjusted in real-time based on traffic patterns, user demands, and application behaviors.

Ultimately, the choice between best effort and guaranteed delivery models depends on the specific requirements of the network and its users. While best effort may still suffice for casual web browsing and background tasks, guaranteed delivery or its approximations are necessary for delivering high-quality real-time services. As digital interactions become more immersive, time-sensitive, and dependent on uninterrupted connectivity, the ability to implement and manage QoS models becomes an essential skill for network architects and administrators. Whether in enterprise data centers, service provider backbones, or wireless access networks, the proper application of QoS principles ensures that every type of traffic gets the treatment it deserves, enabling a seamless and responsive digital experience.

Chapter 6: Integrated Services (IntServ) Model

The Integrated Services, or IntServ, model represents one of the earliest and most comprehensive attempts to provide true Quality of Service guarantees on IP networks. Developed in the mid-1990s by the Internet Engineering Task Force, IntServ was designed to address the growing need for reliable and predictable delivery of data in an increasingly complex digital world. As the Internet began supporting applications such as voice over IP, video conferencing, and real-time data exchange, the limitations of the best-effort model became evident. IntServ was introduced as a solution to provide end-to-end guarantees on bandwidth, delay, jitter, and packet loss, creating a framework that could support sensitive and time-critical communications with the precision previously available only in circuit-switched networks.

At the heart of the IntServ model is the concept of per-flow resource reservation. Unlike models that treat traffic in aggregate or by class, IntServ tracks and manages individual flows, ensuring that each one receives the network resources it needs. A flow in this context is defined as a stream of packets between a specific source and destination, often associated with a particular application or session. This level of granularity allows for precise control over how each flow is treated, making it possible to deliver guaranteed levels of service that can be tailored to the needs of each application.

To enable this per-flow control, IntServ relies on the Resource Reservation Protocol, or RSVP. RSVP is a signaling protocol that allows a host to request a specific Quality of Service from the network before a data stream begins. The host sends an RSVP message along the intended path of the flow, and each router along the path examines the request to determine whether it has sufficient resources to accommodate the flow. If every router can meet the request, they all reserve the necessary resources and send an acknowledgment back to the sender. This process establishes a reserved path through the network where the flow can proceed with the guaranteed service parameters.

RSVP also handles the maintenance and eventual teardown of reservations. It supports both soft state and refresh mechanisms, meaning that reservations must be periodically renewed or they will expire. This helps maintain the flexibility of IP networks while still enabling stateful resource management. However, the requirement for routers to keep state information for each active flow introduces a significant scalability challenge. In small networks or those with limited numbers of flows, this overhead may be acceptable. But in large-scale environments like the public Internet, maintaining per-flow state can consume substantial memory and processing power, potentially degrading router performance and limiting overall scalability.

Despite these limitations, the IntServ model provides strong theoretical guarantees. By combining RSVP signaling with classification, admission control, and traffic policing, IntServ can ensure that flows are admitted only if sufficient resources are available. This prevents oversubscription and ensures that existing flows are not degraded by new traffic. Additionally, IntServ supports various service types, including guaranteed service for applications that require strict bounds on delay and controlled-load service for those that need consistent but not rigid performance. This flexibility makes IntServ suitable for a wide range of use cases, from video streaming to telemedicine.

One of the key advantages of IntServ is its ability to provide deterministic service in environments where performance is critical. For instance, in industrial control systems, financial trading platforms, or remote surgery applications, the ability to guarantee low delay and high reliability is not just desirable but essential. IntServ's detailed reservation mechanism offers a level of assurance that cannot be matched by simpler QoS models. It also lays the foundation for building truly converged networks, where diverse services can coexist on a single infrastructure without compromising on performance.

Nevertheless, the operational complexity of IntServ has limited its widespread deployment. The need to deploy RSVP across all routers along a flow's path, combined with the per-flow state requirements, means that IntServ is best suited for managed networks with centralized control and well-defined traffic patterns. Service providers, for instance, might use IntServ in backbone networks or for premium services that justify the additional resource investment. Enterprises might implement IntServ in segments of the network dedicated to high-priority or latency-sensitive workloads. But for the general Internet, where traffic is dynamic and often unpredictable, the model's scalability issues make it difficult to implement on a large scale.

As networking technologies have advanced, new models such as Differentiated Services and Multiprotocol Label Switching have emerged to address the scalability and operational concerns associated with IntServ. These models sacrifice some of the granularity and guarantees of IntServ in exchange for greater flexibility and efficiency. Even so, IntServ remains a foundational concept in the study and practice of Quality of Service. It represents a gold standard for what is possible in terms of resource reservation and deterministic delivery, and its influence can be seen in the design of more recent QoS frameworks.

The integration of IntServ with other technologies has also been explored. For instance, in hybrid models, IntServ might be used at the edge of the network to reserve resources for critical applications, while core routers use a simplified model like DiffServ to manage aggregate traffic. This allows networks to benefit from the precision of IntServ where it is most needed without incurring its full complexity at scale. There have also been proposals to use software-defined networking to implement IntServ-like functions more efficiently, leveraging centralized control to manage flow state and reservations dynamically.

While IntServ may not be the default model in most networks, its conceptual clarity and rigorous approach to Quality of Service continue to inform network architecture and design. It highlights the importance of planning, resource awareness, and control in delivering high-performance network services. As the demand for real-time, high-reliability applications continues to grow, the principles behind IntServ remain relevant, reminding network engineers of the trade-offs between precision and scalability, and of the value of designing systems that can provide not just connectivity, but predictable, consistent, and assured service.

Chapter 7: Differentiated Services (DiffServ) Model

The Differentiated Services model, commonly referred to as DiffServ, emerged as a scalable and efficient alternative to the Integrated Services (IntServ) model for implementing Quality of Service in IP networks. As networking demands increased, it became clear that the per-flow reservation and state maintenance required by IntServ would not scale effectively in large or highly dynamic environments. DiffServ was designed to address this limitation by simplifying the QoS model while still providing differentiated treatment for different types of traffic. Instead of making individual resource reservations for each flow, DiffServ classifies and aggregates traffic into a limited set of behavior classes, each receiving specific forwarding treatment throughout the network.

DiffServ works by applying traffic classification and marking policies at the edge of the network, typically at the ingress point of an administrative domain. Once packets are marked, they carry their QoS designation throughout the network in the Differentiated Services Code Point (DSCP) field of the IP header. This six-bit field enables the definition of up to sixty-four distinct traffic classes, although in practice, networks commonly use a smaller, standardized subset of these values. These markings determine how each packet is treated as it traverses the network core, influencing queuing, scheduling, and dropping behavior on each hop.

One of the core ideas behind DiffServ is the concept of Per-Hop Behaviors, or PHBs. A PHB defines how packets of a particular class are handled by routers. The most common PHBs include Expedited Forwarding, Assured Forwarding, and Best Effort. Expedited Forwarding is designed for low-latency, low-loss, and low-jitter traffic such as voice and real-time video. It is typically implemented using priority queuing to ensure that this traffic is forwarded before other types. Assured Forwarding provides a more flexible treatment with multiple classes and drop precedence levels, suitable for applications that need reliable delivery but can tolerate some delay. Best Effort, the default behavior, is used for all traffic that has not been explicitly marked for preferential treatment and corresponds to traditional IP delivery without QoS guarantees.

The architecture of DiffServ is fundamentally decentralized. Unlike IntServ, which requires signaling protocols like RSVP and state maintenance on every router, DiffServ relies on pre-configured policies and simple packet inspection at each hop. Routers do not maintain per-flow state and do not need to engage in complex negotiations. Instead, they execute defined forwarding behaviors based on the DSCP values in the packet headers. This stateless approach significantly reduces complexity and allows DiffServ to scale effectively across large networks, including service provider backbones and the public Internet.

Policy enforcement and traffic conditioning in DiffServ are typically carried out at the network edge. This includes classification, marking, policing, and shaping of traffic to ensure it conforms to the expected profiles. Policing involves dropping or remarking packets that exceed agreed-upon thresholds, while shaping delays packets to smooth out bursts. These mechanisms help ensure that traffic entering the network does not overwhelm resources or degrade the performance of other flows. Once traffic is conditioned and marked appropriately, the core of the network can treat it according to the intended service class with minimal processing overhead.

DiffServ supports both relative and absolute QoS models. In a relative model, different traffic classes are treated differently but without strict performance guarantees. For example, voice traffic might receive higher priority than email, but the network does not promise a specific delay or loss rate. In contrast, an absolute model can define precise service level objectives for each class, often enforced through network engineering and provisioning. The ability to support both models makes DiffServ adaptable to a wide range of deployment scenarios, from enterprise networks to cloud data centers and wide-area transport networks.

One of the key strengths of DiffServ lies in its flexibility. Network operators can define their own traffic classes and policies based on organizational needs, application priorities, or business models. For example, an enterprise might assign high priority to business-critical applications like ERP or video conferencing, while deprioritizing bulk data transfers and social media traffic. A service provider might offer differentiated service tiers to customers, charging premium rates for traffic that receives better treatment. The modular design of DiffServ allows it to be integrated into existing IP networks with minimal disruption, making it a practical solution for upgrading network performance without a complete overhaul.

Despite its advantages, DiffServ is not without challenges. One of the main concerns is the lack of end-to-end QoS guarantees across multiple administrative domains. Because DiffServ relies on locally defined policies and does not include a signaling mechanism, coordinating QoS treatment between different networks requires bilateral agreements and policy alignment. This makes it difficult to ensure consistent service levels across the global Internet, especially for applications that span multiple networks. Some providers address this issue through Service Level Agreements, which specify performance metrics and responsibilities, but these agreements can be complex to negotiate and enforce.

Another challenge lies in maintaining fairness and avoiding abuse. Since packet marking is performed at the edge, there is potential for misbehavior if users or devices mark their traffic incorrectly to gain higher priority. To prevent this, networks must implement robust policing mechanisms that verify and enforce marking policies. Similarly, congestion management in the network core must be carefully designed to avoid starvation of lower-priority traffic. Techniques such as weighted fair queuing and random early detection help balance traffic loads and maintain overall network stability.

DiffServ is also evolving to meet the needs of modern network environments. With the rise of software-defined networking and network function virtualization, QoS policies can now be dynamically adjusted based on real-time data and application requirements. This programmability allows for more granular and responsive QoS management, enhancing the capabilities of DiffServ in cloud-native and multi-tenant architectures. Additionally, the integration of DiffServ with newer transport protocols and overlay networks, such as MPLS and segment routing, extends its reach and effectiveness in managing complex traffic flows.

In the context of Quality of Service, the DiffServ model represents a practical balance between scalability and performance. While it may not provide the strict guarantees of the IntServ model, it offers a powerful framework for prioritizing traffic and optimizing resource utilization in large and dynamic networks. By enabling differentiated treatment of traffic based on application needs and business policies, DiffServ allows networks to deliver better experiences to users, improve operational efficiency, and support a wide variety of digital services with varying performance requirements. Its continued relevance in today's networking landscape underscores its importance as a cornerstone of modern QoS implementations.

Chapter 8: Traffic Types and QoS Requirements

In a modern IP network, traffic is far from homogeneous. Different applications and services generate data with distinct characteristics and performance expectations. The way this traffic behaves on the network, and the experience it delivers to users, depends greatly on how it is managed. Understanding the various traffic types and their respective Quality of Service requirements is fundamental to designing a network that supports diverse services without compromising reliability, efficiency, or user satisfaction. Not all data is equal in the eyes of performance. Some traffic types can tolerate delay or jitter, while others require consistent, real-time transmission. Quality of

Service mechanisms are the tools that allow networks to recognize these differences and act accordingly.

One of the most prominent and demanding traffic types is real-time voice communication, typically delivered through Voice over IP. Voice traffic is characterized by small, constant bit rate packets that are highly sensitive to latency, jitter, and packet loss. Even minor interruptions can result in noticeable degradation such as choppy audio, echo, or silence. Human perception is particularly sensitive to the fluidity of conversation, making consistent packet delivery within tight delay bounds essential. For voice applications, end-to-end latency should generally remain under 150 milliseconds to maintain a natural conversation flow. Jitter must be minimized to ensure that packets arrive in the correct timing sequence. QoS for voice traffic prioritizes low-latency delivery paths and often utilizes expedited forwarding treatment to move voice packets through the network as quickly as possible.

Closely related to voice is video traffic, which has become ubiquitous through conferencing platforms, live broadcasts, and streaming services. Video is typically more tolerant of delay than voice, especially in on-demand streaming scenarios where buffering can mitigate the impact of network fluctuations. However, live and interactive video, such as video calls or webinars, shares many of the same sensitivities as voice. It requires consistent throughput and low jitter to prevent pixelation, freezing, or loss of synchronization between audio and video tracks. Packet loss also degrades video quality, particularly for highly compressed formats that depend on predictive encoding. Unlike voice, video streams often require higher bandwidth, especially at high resolutions and frame rates. QoS for video must ensure adequate bandwidth reservation and jitter control, typically through a combination of traffic shaping, priority queuing, and congestion avoidance techniques.

Another important category is transactional data, often generated by enterprise applications such as databases, financial systems, or authentication services. This type of traffic generally involves short bursts of data that must be delivered quickly and reliably. Although less sensitive to jitter, transactional traffic demands low latency and minimal loss to ensure responsive performance and data integrity. In sectors like finance or healthcare, where transactional traffic can represent critical operations, delays or errors can have significant consequences. This traffic is usually given high priority, but not as high as real-time media, to strike a balance between responsiveness and overall network fairness.

Bulk data transfers, such as file downloads, software updates, or backups, represent a very different kind of traffic. These activities typically involve large volumes of data and can consume substantial bandwidth, but they are not time-sensitive. Because they are delay-tolerant, they are generally assigned a lower priority in QoS policies. However, their impact on the network cannot be ignored. If left unmanaged, bulk transfers can saturate links and degrade the performance of more sensitive applications. QoS mechanisms often include rate limiting or traffic shaping to control the impact of bulk traffic, ensuring that it does not interfere with higher-priority services while still allowing the transfer to proceed during periods of low congestion.

Web traffic, including browsing and interactive websites, falls somewhere in the middle of the QoS spectrum. It is generally not as delay-sensitive as voice or video, but users expect fast page loads and responsive interfaces. Latency and packet loss can affect the user experience, especially on dynamic websites that require multiple round trips to load content. Web traffic can also exhibit bursty behavior, with short periods of high activity followed by idle times. This variability makes it challenging to classify and prioritize accurately. QoS policies often treat interactive web traffic with moderate priority, relying on intelligent traffic classification to distinguish between critical web applications and background browsing.

Cloud-based services have introduced new complexities to traffic classification and QoS requirements. Applications like hosted desktops, online collaboration tools, and virtualized environments generate a mix of traffic types, including real-time media, transactional data, and bulk file access. These services depend on consistent performance to maintain usability and productivity. The dynamic nature of cloud traffic requires flexible QoS policies that can adapt to shifting patterns and usage contexts. In many cases, application-aware traffic classification is used to recognize cloud services and assign appropriate service levels. This often involves deep packet inspection or integration with application-layer controllers that provide context beyond simple IP or port-based rules.

Internet of Things devices contribute another layer of diversity to network traffic. IoT traffic is typically characterized by small, frequent data transmissions. While not all IoT applications require stringent QoS, many do. For example, smart grid systems, industrial automation, and remote monitoring often depend on timely and reliable data delivery. Latency or packet loss in these contexts can result in operational delays, system errors, or even safety risks. QoS for IoT often focuses on ensuring that control and telemetry data is prioritized over background processes. In some cases, networks use lightweight QoS mechanisms that suit the limited capabilities of IoT devices, such as priority tagging and simplified classification rules.

Interactive applications such as online gaming and remote desktop services are yet another type of traffic with unique QoS needs. These applications require low latency and high responsiveness to deliver a smooth user experience. Any noticeable delay between user input and system response can render the application frustrating or unusable. Jitter and packet loss must also be minimized to maintain the integrity of the experience, particularly in fast-paced gaming environments. QoS policies for interactive applications often allocate medium to high priority and employ techniques like low-latency queuing and congestion avoidance to support real-time responsiveness.

Network control and signaling traffic, such as routing updates, DNS queries, or authentication handshakes, are essential for the functioning of the network itself. Although this traffic is typically low in volume, its importance is critical. Any disruption or delay in control traffic can cause instability, slow performance, or outages. Therefore, it is common practice to assign high priority to control plane traffic, ensuring that it is transmitted reliably even during times of congestion. Effective QoS strategies recognize the importance of maintaining the integrity of the control plane and allocate resources accordingly.

The diversity of traffic types in modern networks underscores the necessity of robust and adaptable Quality of Service mechanisms. Each category of traffic presents unique demands on the network, and treating all traffic equally inevitably leads to suboptimal performance for critical applications. By accurately identifying traffic types and understanding their respective QoS requirements, network administrators can design and implement policies that ensure performance, fairness, and efficiency across the board. This granular approach to traffic management is what allows networks to meet the complex and evolving demands of users, applications, and services in the digital age.

Chapter 9: Understanding Network Congestion

Network congestion is a phenomenon that occurs when the volume of data traffic surpasses the available capacity of a network or one of its components. It is a condition that degrades the performance and reliability of data transmission, affecting user experience and potentially disrupting services that rely on timely delivery. Understanding the causes, symptoms, and consequences of congestion is fundamental to designing effective Quality of Service policies and maintaining optimal network operation. As networks have evolved to support more users, applications, and devices, the complexity of managing congestion has increased, requiring a deeper comprehension of how data flows through the infrastructure and how resources are consumed.

Congestion typically arises when the rate at which data enters a network segment exceeds the rate at which it can be processed or forwarded. This can happen at any point in the network, whether on a local area network switch, a wide-area router, a wireless access point, or even an endpoint device. The mismatch in speeds or processing capabilities creates queues, where packets wait for their turn to be transmitted. As these queues grow, the delay experienced by each packet increases. Eventually, if the congestion persists, queues may fill up entirely, leading to packet drops. These drops trigger retransmissions and further contribute to the traffic load, creating a feedback loop that can exacerbate the problem.

One of the primary causes of network congestion is the lack of coordination between senders and the network. Most applications, particularly those using the Transmission Control Protocol, are designed to send data as quickly as possible until they encounter resistance in the form of dropped packets or increased delay. While TCP includes congestion control mechanisms to back off when packet loss is detected, these mechanisms react to congestion after it has occurred, rather than preventing it. In high-speed networks or networks with large buffers, the delay before a reaction can lead to a phenomenon known as bufferbloat, where excessive queuing leads to unacceptable latency and jitter even though no packets are being dropped.

Congestion can also be triggered by bursty traffic patterns. Applications such as video streaming, file downloads, and cloud synchronization often send large amounts of data in short bursts, which can momentarily overwhelm intermediate devices. Even if the average load is within acceptable limits, the instantaneous spike in traffic can fill buffers and cause temporary congestion. Similarly, denial-of-service attacks or misconfigured systems can flood the network with traffic, consuming resources and preventing legitimate communication. These scenarios highlight the importance of managing not just total bandwidth but also traffic patterns and burst behavior.

Wireless networks are particularly vulnerable to congestion due to their shared medium and variable link quality. In Wi-Fi networks, all devices on the same channel must compete for airtime. As more devices connect and generate traffic, contention increases, leading to delays and retransmissions. Environmental factors such as interference from other wireless networks, physical obstacles, or even microwave ovens can further degrade performance. In such environments, congestion can become chronic, and without proper management, network usability can decline significantly. Implementing Quality of Service on wireless networks requires special attention to airtime fairness, signal strength, and adaptive bandwidth allocation.

Another critical factor in congestion is the asymmetric nature of many internet connections. In typical residential or small business environments, download speeds are significantly higher than upload speeds. When multiple users attempt to upload data simultaneously, such as during video conferencing or cloud backups, the limited upstream bandwidth can quickly become saturated. This not only affects the quality of the uploading applications but can also impact downstream traffic due to increased latency and queuing at the bottleneck. Understanding the bidirectional nature of traffic and the implications of asymmetry is essential for effective congestion management.

Detecting and diagnosing congestion involves monitoring key performance indicators such as latency, packet loss, jitter, and throughput. A sudden increase in round-trip time, frequent retransmissions, or inconsistent application performance can all signal the presence of congestion. Tools such as ping, traceroute, and flow monitoring provide insight into where congestion may be occurring, whether at the local gateway, within the ISP's network, or on the broader internet. Sophisticated monitoring platforms can correlate traffic patterns with performance metrics, enabling administrators to pinpoint congestion sources and make informed decisions about capacity planning or policy adjustments.

Managing congestion requires a combination of strategies that include traffic prioritization, rate limiting, and intelligent queuing. Quality of Service plays a central role by allowing critical traffic to bypass congestion when necessary. Techniques such as Class-Based Weighted Fair Queuing and Low Latency Queuing ensure that voice and real-time data are transmitted promptly even under heavy load. Traffic shaping smooths out bursts, reducing the likelihood of sudden spikes that overwhelm buffers. Policing enforces bandwidth limits and prevents non-compliant traffic from consuming more than its fair share of resources.

Capacity planning is another essential aspect of congestion management. As usage grows, network infrastructure must be evaluated and upgraded to keep pace with demand. This involves not only increasing link speeds and processing capabilities but also optimizing network design to eliminate chokepoints and reduce latency. Redundancy, load balancing, and segmentation help distribute traffic more evenly and prevent localized congestion from affecting the entire network. In cloud environments, autoscaling and dynamic resource allocation enable networks to adapt to fluctuating loads without manual intervention.

Emerging technologies such as Software-Defined Networking and Network Function Virtualization provide new tools for addressing congestion. By decoupling the control plane from the data plane, SDN enables centralized visibility and policy enforcement, allowing networks to respond dynamically to congestion events. NFV allows for flexible deployment of network services that can be scaled and relocated based on traffic demands. These technologies support real-time analytics and automated responses, shifting congestion management from reactive to proactive.

Understanding network congestion is not only about recognizing when and where it occurs but also about anticipating how changes in usage, application behavior, and infrastructure affect overall performance. As networks become more integral to every aspect of business, education, entertainment, and communication, the ability to manage congestion effectively becomes a defining factor in delivering consistent, high-quality service. Through careful analysis, strategic design, and adaptive management, networks can minimize the impact of congestion and ensure that users and applications receive the performance they require.

Chapter 10: Metrics of QoS: Latency, Jitter, Loss, and Bandwidth

Quality of Service in IP networks is fundamentally about ensuring that data flows through the network in a way that meets the specific requirements of different applications. To do this effectively, it is essential to understand the core metrics that define network performance. These metrics—latency, jitter, packet loss, and bandwidth—form the basis upon which QoS policies are developed, applied, and evaluated. Each metric captures a distinct dimension of the user experience, and their interplay determines whether an application functions smoothly or suffers from delays, interruptions, or data corruption. By measuring, monitoring, and managing these metrics, network administrators can shape traffic behavior to align with service expectations and technical constraints.

Latency refers to the time it takes for a data packet to travel from the source to the destination across the network. This delay can be influenced by various factors, including the physical distance between endpoints, the number of intermediate devices such as routers and switches, the processing time at each hop, and the queuing delay caused by congestion. Latency is typically measured in milliseconds and has a profound impact on applications that rely on real-time communication. For example, voice calls and video conferencing require low latency to preserve the natural rhythm of human interaction. Even small delays can make conversations feel disjointed or lead to people talking over each other. In online gaming and remote desktop sessions, high latency translates into sluggish controls and poor responsiveness, severely affecting usability.

Latency is not a fixed value but rather a dynamic measure that can vary depending on traffic conditions and network topology. Tools such as ping or traceroute can provide round-trip latency values, which represent the total time for a packet to travel from source to destination and back. For one-way latency, specialized monitoring tools are required. In QoS planning, acceptable latency thresholds depend on the application. Voice is typically considered acceptable up to 150 milliseconds, while video may tolerate slightly more. Data applications such as email or file transfers are more tolerant but can still be negatively affected by excessive delays in certain contexts.

Closely related to latency is jitter, which refers to the variation in packet arrival times. Even if average latency is within acceptable limits, irregularities in the timing of packet delivery can disrupt the performance of time-sensitive applications. Jitter is especially problematic for voice and video streams that rely on a consistent flow of data to maintain quality. When packets arrive out of order or with fluctuating delays, the receiving application may experience gaps, artifacts, or buffering. To mitigate jitter, many real-time applications implement jitter buffers that temporarily store incoming packets and release them at regular intervals. However, this buffering introduces additional latency and is only effective within certain bounds. Beyond a certain threshold, jitter becomes unmanageable and degrades the user experience.

Jitter is often caused by network congestion, where competing flows create delays and uneven queuing times. It can also result from routing changes, varying path lengths, or device-level interruptions such as CPU spikes or interface resets. Measuring jitter typically involves analyzing the time difference between successive packets in a stream and calculating the average deviation. Minimizing jitter requires careful traffic engineering, prioritization of real-time traffic, and adequate provisioning of network resources. QoS policies that include low-latency queuing and traffic shaping are essential tools for managing jitter in busy or unpredictable environments.

Packet loss occurs when one or more packets fail to reach their intended destination. This can happen due to buffer overflows in routers, physical layer errors, software bugs, or network congestion. While some degree of packet loss is inevitable in any network, excessive loss severely impacts application performance. Real-time applications like voice and video are particularly sensitive because lost packets are not retransmitted. The result is audible glitches, frozen frames, or distorted images. In contrast, applications that use TCP, such as web browsing or file downloads, detect packet loss and retransmit lost data. While this ensures data integrity, it also increases overall latency and reduces throughput.

Packet loss is typically expressed as a percentage of total packets sent, and acceptable levels vary by application. Voice can generally tolerate up to 1% loss before quality noticeably degrades, while video may handle up to 2% depending on compression and buffering. For data applications, even small losses can cause significant slowdowns due to repeated retransmissions. Detecting and diagnosing packet loss involves tools such as ICMP tests, flow analysis, and error counters on network interfaces. QoS strategies to minimize packet loss include congestion management techniques like Random Early Detection, proper traffic classification, and ensuring that high-priority traffic has sufficient resources during peak usage periods.

Bandwidth represents the maximum amount of data that can be transmitted over a network link in a given period, usually measured in bits per second. While often conflated with speed, bandwidth is more accurately described as capacity. It defines how much data can flow through the network at once and directly affects the performance of bandwidth-intensive applications like video streaming, large downloads, and cloud-based backups. Insufficient bandwidth leads to congestion, increased latency, and higher packet loss, especially when multiple high-demand applications operate simultaneously. Allocating bandwidth appropriately ensures that critical services receive the necessary resources to function properly.

Unlike latency or loss, bandwidth is a finite resource that must be shared among all users and applications. During periods of high demand, bandwidth contention becomes a major source of performance issues. QoS mechanisms help manage bandwidth through policies that limit, prioritize, or reserve capacity for specific types of traffic. Traffic shaping, for instance, controls the rate of outgoing traffic to match the available bandwidth, while policing enforces strict limits on flows that exceed their allocated share. Load balancing across multiple links or paths can also help distribute bandwidth demand more evenly, preventing bottlenecks and improving overall efficiency.

These four metrics—latency, jitter, loss, and bandwidth—are not isolated. They interact in complex ways and influence one another under different network conditions. A high-bandwidth link may still suffer from high latency if it is geographically long or poorly managed. Low latency may still be inadequate if jitter causes delivery inconsistency. Packet loss may remain hidden until network usage spikes or until a sensitive application reveals the degradation. Therefore, QoS strategies must be holistic, addressing all four metrics in tandem to create a stable and high-performing network environment.

In real-world implementations, continuous monitoring of these metrics is essential. Network performance can fluctuate throughout the day based on user behavior, application usage, and external factors. Effective QoS relies not only on setting policies but also on adapting to changing conditions through dynamic configuration and intelligent automation. By maintaining visibility into latency, jitter, loss, and bandwidth, administrators can proactively identify emerging issues, fine-tune policies, and ensure that service quality aligns with user expectations and business objectives. These metrics are the foundation of every QoS decision and the key indicators of network health in a connected world.

Chapter 11: Packet Classification Basics

Packet classification is a foundational component of Quality of Service in IP networks. It is the process by which network devices identify and categorize incoming packets so that they can be treated according to predefined policies. This categorization is essential because different types of traffic have different requirements in terms of latency, jitter, bandwidth, and reliability. Without the ability to distinguish between packets, a network cannot apply any meaningful QoS policies, and all traffic must be treated equally under the best-effort delivery model. As networks have become more complex and traffic more diverse, packet classification has evolved from simple static rules to sophisticated and dynamic mechanisms capable of understanding the context and purpose of data flows.

At its most basic level, packet classification involves inspecting the header of each packet to extract information such as the source and destination IP address, source and destination port number, and the protocol in use. These five elements are commonly referred to as the five-tuple and provide a straightforward way to identify traffic flows. For example, a packet with a source port of 5060 and using the UDP protocol is likely part of a VoIP session. Similarly, TCP traffic on port 443 can be identified as HTTPS. By matching these attributes against a set of classification rules, the device can determine how the packet should be treated.

However, relying solely on the five-tuple is not always sufficient, particularly in modern networks where applications often use dynamic ports or encapsulate traffic in encrypted tunnels. In such cases, more advanced classification methods are required. These may include deep packet inspection, which examines the payload of the packet to identify application signatures, or behavioral analysis that considers the context of traffic patterns over time. While deep packet inspection provides a much higher level of accuracy, it is also more resource-intensive and may raise privacy and performance concerns. Therefore, network architects must carefully balance the need for precise classification with the constraints of processing capacity and policy requirements.

Once a packet is classified, it is typically marked with a specific value that denotes its category or priority. This marking is applied to specific fields in the packet header, such as the Differentiated Services Code Point in the IP header or the Class of Service field in Ethernet frames. These markings serve as indicators to downstream devices, telling them how to handle the packet without needing to reclassify it. In this way, classification and marking work together to create an end-to-end QoS policy that can be consistently enforced across the entire network path.

The effectiveness of packet classification depends on the accuracy and specificity of the rules that define it. Rules must be granular enough to distinguish between different applications and services but not so numerous that they become unmanageable. For example, separating video conferencing traffic from bulk data transfers is essential because they have different QoS requirements. However, trying to distinguish between every individual application on a network may lead to a bloated rule set that is difficult to maintain and prone to errors. Administrators must therefore design classification schemes that reflect the organization's priorities and the types of applications in use, often grouping similar applications into classes with shared QoS treatment.

Packet classification is typically implemented at the network edge, where devices such as routers, switches, and firewalls examine incoming traffic and apply the initial categorization. Edge classification is crucial because it sets the tone for how traffic will be handled as it moves through the network. Once traffic is marked at the edge, core devices in the network can simply read the markings and apply the corresponding forwarding behaviors. This division of labor allows the core to remain stateless and efficient, focusing solely on high-speed forwarding while the more complex classification logic is executed at the periphery.

In addition to static rules, packet classification can also be dynamic, adapting in real time based on traffic conditions or user behavior. For example, a network management system might detect a video call in progress and dynamically reclassify its packets for higher priority handling. Similarly, traffic generated by a specific user or device might be reclassified based on time of day, location, or policy changes. This dynamic approach requires integration with policy engines and real-time monitoring systems, enabling the network to respond intelligently to changing demands.

Policy-based routing is another technique that relies heavily on packet classification. In this approach, packets are routed based on their classification rather than traditional destination-based metrics. For example, high-priority traffic might be routed over a low-latency path, while background traffic takes a less congested route. This selective forwarding allows organizations to optimize their network resources and ensure that critical services receive the performance they require. Packet classification thus becomes the enabler of differentiated routing strategies that align with business objectives.

Security is also enhanced by effective packet classification. By identifying and isolating traffic types, the network can enforce security policies more precisely. For example, unauthorized peer-to-peer traffic can be blocked or redirected, while traffic from sensitive applications can be monitored more closely. Classification enables segmentation, allowing administrators to define zones of trust and control how data flows between them. In this context, packet classification is not just about performance but also about compliance, governance, and risk management.

In wireless and mobile networks, packet classification faces additional challenges. Limited bandwidth, variable signal strength, and user mobility introduce fluctuations in traffic behavior that can complicate classification efforts. Devices may roam between access points, switch between networks, or change their traffic patterns based on environmental factors. To cope with this, wireless QoS frameworks often include mechanisms for classification based on media access control addresses, session information, or predefined traffic types like voice or video. These classification methods help maintain service quality in environments where traditional identifiers may be less stable.

The future of packet classification lies in greater automation and intelligence. As networks adopt machine learning and AI-driven analytics, classification can become more adaptive, learning from traffic patterns and improving accuracy over time. Instead of relying solely on static rule sets, future systems may use predictive models to anticipate application behavior and preemptively assign appropriate QoS classes. This evolution will make packet classification more resilient to change, more responsive to user needs, and more aligned with the goals of digital transformation.

Packet classification is not a one-time task but an ongoing process that must evolve alongside the network and the applications it supports. It is the first step in applying QoS and a critical determinant of how well a network can meet the diverse and demanding needs of modern users. By accurately identifying and categorizing traffic, networks gain the ability to allocate resources wisely, prioritize critical services, and maintain a consistent and high-quality experience across all types of applications. Whether implemented through simple access control lists or complex behavioral algorithms, packet classification remains one of the most powerful tools in the QoS toolbox.

Chapter 12: Deep Packet Inspection for QoS

Deep Packet Inspection, or DPI, is a powerful and increasingly essential technology in the implementation of Quality of Service within IP networks. Unlike basic packet classification methods that rely solely on the header information of network packets, DPI goes further by examining the actual payload, or content, of the data being transmitted. This deeper level of analysis allows for more accurate identification of applications, services, and user behaviors, enabling administrators to apply precise QoS policies based on what the traffic actually is, rather than just where it is going or which port it is using. As applications become more complex, encrypted, and dynamic, the limitations of traditional packet classification methods become evident, making DPI a critical tool for maintaining visibility and control over network performance.

DPI operates by scanning the entire packet, including both the header and the payload, to extract detailed information about its contents. This can include application signatures, file types, protocol patterns, metadata, and even keywords or data formats. The inspection engine uses this information to match the packet against a database of known patterns, identifying the specific application or service generating the traffic. For example, while traditional classification may only identify traffic as TCP on port 443, DPI can determine whether that traffic belongs to a video conferencing session, a banking transaction, or a social media app running over HTTPS. This level of granularity enables QoS policies to be far more effective and tailored to real-world usage.

The accuracy of DPI is one of its greatest strengths. By recognizing traffic based on actual content rather than relying on static port numbers or IP addresses, DPI can classify modern applications that use dynamic ports, encapsulation, or tunneling techniques. Many applications today are designed to evade basic classification methods, either to improve performance through load balancing and encryption or to avoid detection in environments with strict traffic controls. DPI overcomes these challenges by looking inside the packet, making it possible to identify and manage traffic types that would otherwise go unnoticed or be misclassified. This is particularly important in environments with strict performance or compliance requirements, where precise control over traffic behavior is necessary.

In the context of QoS, DPI enables differentiated service treatment at an unprecedented level. Once traffic is identified accurately, it can be assigned to a specific service class, marked appropriately, and directed through the network with policies that reflect its importance and performance sensitivity. Real-time communications can be prioritized, bulk data transfers can be shaped or delayed, and potentially disruptive traffic can be limited or redirected. This capability is crucial in converged networks where multiple services share the same infrastructure and bandwidth must be allocated dynamically based on real-time demands.

DPI also supports more advanced policy enforcement strategies. For example, bandwidth can be allocated not just by application type but by user, device, or even session. A single user watching a video stream for entertainment might be assigned a lower priority than another user participating in a live video conference for work purposes. DPI makes it possible to differentiate between these scenarios by identifying context and applying policies accordingly. This level of control leads to more efficient use of network resources, improved user experience for critical applications, and reduced risk of congestion or service degradation.

Security is another area where DPI contributes to QoS. By inspecting packet content, DPI can detect anomalies, unauthorized applications, and malicious behavior that might otherwise affect network performance. For instance, a botnet generating outbound spam traffic could consume bandwidth and degrade service for legitimate users. DPI can identify this activity based on content patterns and either block the traffic or assign it to a low-priority queue, preserving the performance of more important services. Similarly, DPI can recognize traffic associated with policy violations, such as peer-to-peer file sharing on a corporate network, and apply enforcement actions that align with organizational policies.

Despite its benefits, DPI is not without challenges. The process of inspecting packets in detail requires significant processing power and memory, especially at high data rates. This can introduce latency or become a bottleneck if not properly managed. Hardware acceleration, distributed inspection architectures, and intelligent sampling techniques are often used to mitigate these performance concerns. Additionally, the increasing use of encryption presents a fundamental obstacle to DPI. When traffic is encrypted end-to-end, the payload is no longer accessible for inspection, limiting DPI's effectiveness. In such cases, some solutions involve decrypting traffic at network boundaries using trusted proxies or inspecting metadata and behavioral patterns rather than content itself.

Privacy is another important consideration with DPI. Because the technology involves inspecting the contents of users' communications, it raises concerns about surveillance and data protection. Regulatory frameworks such as GDPR impose strict requirements on how data can be monitored and stored, and organizations using DPI must ensure they comply with these regulations. Transparent policies, user consent, and data anonymization techniques are essential components of a responsible DPI implementation. The goal is to balance the need for visibility and control with the obligation to protect user rights and confidentiality.

Integration of DPI into modern networking environments has been facilitated by its inclusion in next-generation firewalls, unified threat management systems, and software-defined networking controllers. These platforms leverage DPI for both security and QoS, providing a unified view of network activity and enabling coordinated policy enforcement. In SDN environments, DPI data can feed into centralized control systems that dynamically adjust routing and resource allocation based on real-time traffic classification. This integration enhances agility and scalability, allowing networks to respond quickly to changes in usage patterns or emerging threats.

In cloud and virtualized environments, DPI faces additional complexity due to east-west traffic between virtual machines and containers. Traditional DPI appliances may not have visibility into this internal traffic, necessitating new approaches such as virtual DPI instances, host-based inspection agents, or integration with orchestration platforms. These tools extend the reach of DPI into distributed and ephemeral environments, ensuring that QoS policies remain effective even as the network becomes more abstract and decentralized.

DPI is increasingly enhanced by artificial intelligence and machine learning. By training models on vast datasets of network traffic, these systems can recognize subtle patterns, adapt to new applications, and improve classification accuracy over time. AI-powered DPI can detect previously unknown applications, respond to zero-day behaviors, and fine-tune QoS policies in near real-time. This adaptive capability is essential in a world where applications evolve rapidly and user expectations for performance continue to rise.

Deep Packet Inspection is a critical enabler of advanced Quality of Service strategies in modern IP networks. By providing visibility into the actual content and purpose of network traffic, it allows for precise classification, efficient resource allocation, and effective enforcement of service-level policies. As networks continue to grow in complexity, the role of DPI will only become more central to ensuring performance, security, and user satisfaction in increasingly dynamic and demanding digital environments.

Chapter 13: Access Control Lists and Classification

Access Control Lists, commonly known as ACLs, play a fundamental role in the classification of network traffic for Quality of Service purposes. Originally designed for security, ACLs have evolved into versatile tools for identifying, filtering, and categorizing packets as they traverse a network. When applied in the context of QoS, ACLs become essential building blocks that enable routers and switches to distinguish between traffic types and enforce policies that prioritize, limit, or reroute packets based on their attributes. Although simple in concept, the flexibility and precision of ACLs make them a key component in developing an intelligent and efficient QoS strategy.

At the core of an ACL is a series of rules or statements that match specific characteristics of a packet. These characteristics typically include source and destination IP addresses, protocol types such as TCP or UDP, and port numbers associated with particular services. Each rule defines a match condition, and once a packet meets that condition, an action is applied. In traditional security applications, that action might be to permit or deny the packet. In QoS classification, the action is often to assign the packet to a particular class, mark it with a Differentiated Services Code Point value, or subject it to further inspection or policy enforcement.

ACL-based classification operates at the network layer, making it highly efficient and scalable for high-throughput environments. Because ACLs rely on header information rather than payload content, they can be evaluated quickly with minimal processing overhead. This is especially important in backbone or core networks where traffic volumes are high, and speed is a priority. By leveraging ACLs, network devices can rapidly categorize packets into traffic classes without performing deeper inspection, allowing for real-time classification that keeps pace with modern data rates.

One of the key advantages of using ACLs for QoS classification is the level of control they provide. Network administrators can define detailed rules that match very specific traffic patterns. For example, an ACL can be used to identify all HTTP traffic coming from a particular subnet or prioritize VoIP traffic destined for a specific call server. This granularity allows for precise targeting of QoS policies, ensuring that critical applications receive the appropriate level of service while less important traffic is managed accordingly. ACLs can also be combined with other criteria, such as interface, VLAN, or user identity, to create even more refined classification schemes.

The process of creating ACLs for QoS begins with understanding the traffic profile of the network. Administrators must identify which applications and services are in use, how they behave, and what performance requirements they have. This analysis informs the construction of ACL rules that accurately match traffic types. Once the rules are defined, they are applied to interfaces or access points where traffic enters the network. When a packet arrives, it is compared against the ACL entries in sequential order. The first match determines the classification outcome, and no further entries are evaluated. This sequential nature means that the order of entries in an ACL is critical, and careful planning is required to avoid unintended matches or policy conflicts.

ACLs can be categorized as standard or extended, depending on the level of detail they support. Standard ACLs typically match based on source IP address alone, making them simpler and faster but less flexible. Extended ACLs offer a broader set of matching criteria, including source and destination IP addresses, protocol types, and port numbers. Extended ACLs are more commonly used for QoS because they provide the granularity needed to distinguish between different applications and traffic flows. In some cases, named ACLs or object-based ACLs are used to simplify management by allowing administrators to reference groups of addresses or services rather than listing them individually.

One of the limitations of ACL-based classification is that it relies on static, pre-defined rules. While this provides predictability and consistency, it may not be sufficient in dynamic environments where applications change behavior or use non-standard ports. For example, many modern web applications use encrypted traffic over HTTPS and may not be distinguishable using port numbers alone. In such cases, ACLs must be supplemented with more advanced classification methods such as Deep Packet Inspection or application-aware firewalls. Still, ACLs serve as an efficient first line of classification that can quickly handle the majority of traffic types in a predictable and resource-efficient manner.

In addition to classification, ACLs can also be used to enforce traffic policies by directing packets into specific queues, applying rate limits, or triggering additional processing. For instance, an ACL might identify high-priority voice traffic and place it into a low-latency queue, while identifying bulk file transfers and subjecting them to traffic shaping. These actions are typically implemented through service policies that reference ACLs as their classification mechanism. This modular approach allows for clear separation between traffic identification and traffic treatment, making policies easier to understand, audit, and maintain.

ACLs also play a role in hierarchical QoS configurations, where traffic is classified at multiple levels. In a two-level hierarchy, the first level might classify traffic into broad categories such as voice, video, or data using ACLs. The second level could then further classify traffic within each category based on user, device, or session attributes. This layered classification model provides greater flexibility and allows for more nuanced traffic control. ACLs at the base of the hierarchy ensure that traffic is directed into the correct initial class, forming the foundation upon which more detailed policies can be built.

When used in conjunction with monitoring and analytics tools, ACLs can also provide visibility into traffic patterns and help identify trends or anomalies. For example, by logging matches against specific ACL entries, administrators can gain insight into how much traffic belongs to a particular class or whether unexpected traffic types are appearing. This information is valuable for capacity planning, policy refinement, and security auditing. Over time, the data collected from ACL logs can inform decisions about infrastructure upgrades, application optimization, and changes in network usage.

In virtualized and cloud environments, ACL-based classification must be adapted to function within software-defined infrastructures. Many virtual switches and cloud networking platforms support ACL-like constructs that can be applied programmatically through orchestration tools or APIs. This allows for consistent QoS classification across hybrid environments and enables automation of policy deployment. The principles remain the same—identifying traffic based on defined criteria and applying the appropriate treatment—but the implementation is abstracted into software, increasing agility and scalability.

Access Control Lists continue to be one of the most reliable and versatile tools for traffic classification in QoS. Their simplicity, efficiency, and compatibility with most network devices make them a logical choice for initial traffic identification. While they may not handle every classification scenario, they provide a solid foundation that supports more complex and dynamic QoS strategies. When properly designed and maintained, ACLs enable networks to deliver differentiated services with confidence, ensuring that each type of traffic receives the attention it requires while preserving the overall performance and integrity of the system.

Chapter 14: Traffic Marking Techniques

Traffic marking is a critical element of Quality of Service implementation in IP networks. It refers to the process of tagging packets with specific identifiers that signal their relative importance or required handling behavior as they move through the network. Once marked, these packets can be recognized and treated appropriately by intermediate devices such as routers and switches without needing to perform deep analysis at every hop. Traffic marking serves as the bridge between classification and enforcement, allowing networks to make consistent decisions about packet priority, queuing, policing, or shaping based on predefined policies. This technique is fundamental to achieving efficient, predictable, and scalable QoS in both enterprise and service provider environments.

Marking typically occurs after packet classification, when a packet has already been identified according to criteria such as application type, source and destination addresses, port numbers, or even content inspection. The result of that classification is a decision to assign the packet to a particular class of service. To convey this classification throughout the network, a mark is applied to a specific field in the packet header. This mark travels with the packet, ensuring that each device in the forwarding path understands how to handle the packet in accordance with the established QoS framework. The process of marking is standardized, which allows interoperability between different network devices and vendors.

One of the most widely used marking fields in IP networks is the Differentiated Services Code Point, or DSCP. This six-bit field is part of the IP header and supports up to sixty-four different code points, each representing a specific Per-Hop Behavior. These behaviors can include priority queuing, bandwidth guarantees, or specific drop preferences during congestion. DSCP markings are versatile and provide a scalable solution for modern networks. Once a packet is marked with a DSCP value, routers and switches along the path can reference that value to determine which output queue to use, how much bandwidth to allocate, or whether to forward or drop the packet in case of congestion.

In Layer 2 networks, particularly those based on Ethernet, the Class of Service field is used for traffic marking. This three-bit field resides in the 802.1Q VLAN tag and supports eight levels of priority, from 0 to 7. These priority levels are often mapped to traffic classes such as best effort, background, video, voice, and network control. Layer 2 marking is particularly important in switched environments where IP-based markings are not visible or not enforced. By setting the CoS value, devices can influence the internal queuing and scheduling behavior of Ethernet switches, enabling end-to-end QoS policies even within the LAN.

Another form of marking is applied at the transport layer through the use of MPLS Experimental bits, commonly referred to as the EXP field.

In MPLS networks, labels are used to forward packets based on predetermined paths rather than IP addresses. The EXP field, now known more accurately as the Traffic Class field, allows for up to eight priority levels. This marking mechanism ensures that packets in MPLS environments can still receive differentiated treatment, even when IP headers are not examined. It provides compatibility with existing QoS models and enables service providers to enforce traffic policies across large and complex backbones.

Marking is not limited to network-layer or link-layer headers. Application-layer marking is also gaining importance, particularly in environments that support end-to-end QoS. Modern applications can mark their own traffic using APIs or system-level configuration, signaling their performance requirements directly to the network. For example, a video conferencing application may tag its packets with high-priority markings, indicating a need for low latency and high reliability. This self-marking approach provides greater context for QoS decisions and enables networks to respond dynamically to user needs and application behavior.

The point at which marking occurs in the network is a strategic decision. Ideally, traffic should be marked as close to the source as possible, ensuring that policies are applied consistently throughout the packet's journey. This typically means applying markings at the network edge, such as on access routers, firewalls, or end-user devices. Edge marking establishes the expected handling class before the packet enters the core network, allowing internal devices to operate efficiently using fast path forwarding based on header values. In cases where traffic originates from untrusted sources or where markings cannot be verified, marking may be deferred to a trusted network boundary where packets are reclassified and marked based on enterprise or provider policies.

Trust boundaries are a key concept in marking strategies. Not all markings can be trusted, particularly in environments where users may have the ability to alter packet headers. A device might mark its traffic as high priority in an attempt to gain preferential treatment, potentially disrupting the fairness of the QoS system. To mitigate this risk, networks define trust boundaries and selectively honor or override markings based on policy. For instance, access switches might trust markings from VoIP phones but remark all other traffic to a default value. This ensures that only authorized and accurately classified traffic receives QoS treatment, preserving the integrity and predictability of the network.

Remarking is the process of changing a packet's mark after its initial classification. This may be necessary when traffic crosses administrative domains, moves between different network segments, or requires policy adjustments based on new context. For example, a packet marked as high priority in a branch office may be downgraded to medium priority when entering the core network if bandwidth is more constrained. Remarking provides the flexibility to adapt QoS behavior without requiring reclassification, enabling consistent policy enforcement across diverse environments.

Traffic marking must also be coordinated with queuing and scheduling policies on network devices. A marked packet by itself does not receive preferential treatment unless the device is configured to interpret and act on the marking. This means that marking strategies must be integrated into the overall QoS architecture, with appropriate mapping of DSCP, CoS, or MPLS EXP values to output queues and service levels. Standard mappings exist, such as the IP Precedence to DSCP mapping or DSCP to CoS equivalencies, but each network may define its own class-of-service structure based on business needs and technical capabilities.

Monitoring and auditing marking behavior is vital to ensuring the effectiveness of QoS policies. Network administrators must verify that packets are being marked correctly at the edge, that intermediate devices are honoring those markings, and that the desired service outcomes are being achieved. Tools such as packet capture, flow analysis, and traffic counters help validate that markings are present and being interpreted properly. Discrepancies may indicate configuration errors, misbehaving applications, or policy violations, all of which must be addressed to maintain consistent performance.

Traffic marking techniques represent a key mechanism by which networks enforce differentiated treatment for packets. By embedding classification results into packet headers, marking allows traffic to be managed efficiently across diverse topologies, protocols, and technologies. It provides a consistent, scalable, and interoperable way to deliver Quality of Service, aligning network behavior with the needs of applications, users, and organizations. Through careful design, enforcement at trust boundaries, and continuous monitoring, traffic marking enables modern networks to support the increasing demand for real-time, high-performance, and mission-critical communication.

Chapter 15: DSCP and IP Precedence Values

Differentiated Services Code Point (DSCP) and IP Precedence are two integral components of the Quality of Service architecture used in IP networks to enable traffic differentiation and prioritization. These values are embedded in the IP packet header and serve as indicators for how network devices should treat each packet as it traverses through the network. They provide a standardized method for marking traffic based on priority, ensuring that critical services such as voice, video, and real-time applications receive the necessary resources to perform optimally even in times of congestion. Understanding the structure, use, and relationship between DSCP and IP Precedence values is essential for designing a network that supports efficient and reliable QoS policies.

IP Precedence was introduced in the original specification of IPv4, as part of the Type of Service (ToS) byte in the IP header. The ToS byte was designed to allow packets to carry information about their priority and handling preferences. Within this byte, the first three bits were designated as the IP Precedence field, providing a total of eight possible values ranging from 0 to 7. These values were used to signal the relative importance of packets, with higher numbers indicating higher priority. For example, a packet with a precedence value of 7 was considered network control traffic and given the highest level of attention, while a value of 0 represented best-effort traffic with no special treatment.

Although IP Precedence was a step toward differentiated traffic treatment, it had limitations in terms of granularity and scalability. The three-bit field only allowed for eight levels of priority, which was insufficient for modern networks that needed to distinguish between a wide range of applications with varying QoS requirements.

Furthermore, the semantics of each value were not strictly defined across different vendors or network environments, leading to inconsistent behavior. To address these shortcomings, the Differentiated Services (DiffServ) model was developed, which redefined the use of the ToS byte and introduced the DSCP field as a more flexible and powerful alternative.

DSCP expanded the available classification space by allocating six bits of the redefined ToS byte for code points, allowing for up to 64 distinct traffic classes. This provided the necessary flexibility to support a wide variety of applications and policies. Each DSCP value corresponds to a specific Per-Hop Behavior (PHB), which determines how the packet should be queued, scheduled, and forwarded at each hop in the network. The remaining two bits of the original ToS byte were reserved for future use, currently referred to as Explicit Congestion Notification (ECN) bits, which are used for congestion management rather than classification.

The DSCP field allows network administrators to define multiple service classes with varying levels of priority and performance characteristics. For example, Expedited Forwarding (EF), typically assigned a DSCP value of 46, is used for low-latency, low-loss, and low-jitter services like VoIP. Assured Forwarding (AF) defines a set of service classes with different levels of drop precedence, providing more nuanced handling for important but less time-sensitive traffic. Each AF class has multiple DSCP values, such as AF11, AF12, AF13, representing increasing likelihood of packet drop under congestion. Best-Effort traffic, which does not require any special treatment, is typically marked with a DSCP value of 0.

Despite the introduction of DSCP, many network devices and legacy systems still recognize and use IP Precedence values. To maintain compatibility and ensure seamless interoperability, DSCP values are often mapped to corresponding IP Precedence levels. This mapping allows for a smooth transition from older QoS mechanisms to the more advanced DiffServ model. For example, DSCP values in the range of 0 to 7 align directly with the original IP Precedence values. However, the mapping becomes more complex as DSCP introduces new code points that do not have direct IP Precedence equivalents. In these cases, administrators must define custom mappings that align DSCP-based classifications with existing device behavior and QoS policies.

Configuring DSCP and IP Precedence values involves identifying traffic types, classifying them using access control lists or deep packet inspection, and then applying the appropriate mark to the packet. Once marked, packets are processed by intermediate devices based on the associated PHB. This might involve placing packets in specific output queues, scheduling them for faster transmission, or dropping them under congestion conditions according to their drop precedence. The success of this model depends on consistent interpretation and enforcement of DSCP values across all devices in the traffic path, which is why many organizations adopt QoS standards and profiles that define how each value should be handled.

One of the challenges in using DSCP and IP Precedence effectively is ensuring that markings are trusted and preserved throughout the network. In some environments, packets marked by end-user devices may not be trusted by intermediate devices, leading to remarking or even stripping of QoS values. To prevent this, many networks establish trust boundaries, typically at the edge, where packets are examined and remarked if necessary. Routers and switches within the trusted domain then process the packets based on these verified markings. This model maintains consistency and ensures that only correctly classified traffic receives prioritized treatment.

In enterprise networks, DSCP marking is often used in conjunction with internal class-of-service models to manage traffic across WAN links or between campus segments. For example, a company might define three service classes—voice, business-critical data, and best-effort—and map them to DSCP values of 46, 34, and 0, respectively. These markings inform not only queuing and scheduling decisions within the network but also serve as indicators for service-level agreements with external service providers. Many providers support DSCP-aware services, allowing customers to extend QoS policies beyond their local environment into the broader internet or MPLS backbone.

In service provider environments, DSCP and IP Precedence play a crucial role in delivering differentiated services to customers. By marking traffic at ingress points, providers can ensure that premium traffic receives higher levels of service, while best-effort or non-critical traffic is delivered with standard priority. This supports business models that offer tiered service levels, enabling providers to monetize network performance and guarantee service quality for high-value customers. In these cases, accurate marking, consistent policy enforcement, and coordination across multiple administrative domains are essential for maintaining the integrity of the QoS framework.

The use of DSCP and IP Precedence continues to evolve as networks become more dynamic and application-aware. With the rise of cloud computing, virtualization, and software-defined networking, QoS policies must adapt to changing traffic patterns and user demands. Dynamic marking based on application context, user identity, or device type is becoming more common, supported by orchestration platforms and intelligent network controllers. This shift enhances the relevance of DSCP and IP Precedence, allowing them to serve as flexible and programmable tools for delivering predictable, high-performance network experiences in an increasingly complex digital landscape.

Chapter 16: Class of Service (CoS) in Layer 2

Class of Service, or CoS, is a vital mechanism in Layer 2 networking that allows for traffic differentiation and prioritization before packets are even inspected at the IP layer. While much of the Quality of Service conversation centers on Layer 3 techniques such as DSCP and IP Precedence, CoS operates at the data link layer and plays a critical role in environments where traffic needs to be managed at the switching level, often before routing decisions are made. This is especially relevant in enterprise campus networks, metro Ethernet environments, and data centers where Ethernet is the dominant transmission technology. CoS is implemented using the IEEE 802.1p standard, which defines how Ethernet frames can be tagged with priority information, allowing switches to make forwarding decisions based on traffic importance.

CoS marking is performed using a three-bit field in the 802.1Q VLAN tag. This field, commonly referred to as the Priority Code Point (PCP), supports eight distinct levels of priority, ranging from zero to seven. These levels are not application-specific but can be mapped to traffic classes by network administrators based on organizational needs and traffic profiles. For example, voice traffic might be assigned a CoS value of five, video a value of four, and best-effort traffic a value of zero. These CoS values are interpreted by Layer 2 devices such as Ethernet switches to place frames into different queues, apply specific transmission scheduling algorithms, and ensure that time-sensitive traffic receives expedited handling.

The CoS model does not inherently define what each priority value means. Instead, the interpretation of these values is left to the network design. This flexibility allows for customization but also introduces a risk of inconsistency if policies are not uniformly applied across the infrastructure. In practice, many organizations adopt a standard mapping of CoS values to traffic types, which are then consistently enforced across all Layer 2 devices. This mapping might follow industry best practices or align with internal QoS classifications defined at Layer 3 using DSCP. In such integrated environments, CoS values can be derived from DSCP markings at the network edge and used to maintain traffic differentiation within Layer 2 segments of the network.

Switches that support QoS use CoS values to determine how frames are queued and forwarded internally. This process is known as traffic prioritization or internal QoS. Most enterprise switches have multiple hardware or software queues per port, each assigned to a specific CoS value or range. When frames arrive, the switch examines the PCP field and places each frame into the appropriate queue. During transmission, the switch services these queues based on a defined scheduling algorithm such as strict priority, weighted round robin, or a combination of both. Frames in higher-priority queues are transmitted first, ensuring that delay-sensitive traffic such as VoIP is not held back by lower-priority data such as file transfers or background backups.

Layer 2 CoS is particularly effective in high-speed switching environments where routing decisions are not yet being made or where minimal latency is required. It ensures that even before packets are evaluated at Layer 3, they are already being handled in a way that reflects their importance. This is especially important in collapsed core designs or in metro Ethernet connections where frames traverse multiple switching hops before reaching a Layer 3 boundary. In these cases, the consistent use of CoS values ensures that QoS policies are enforced from the very first switch the frame encounters, reducing the likelihood of congestion and performance degradation in the early stages of transmission.

In addition to prioritizing forwarding behavior, CoS values are also used in traffic policing and shaping at Layer 2. Policing involves measuring the rate of traffic associated with each CoS value and taking action when thresholds are exceeded. For example, a switch might be configured to drop or remark frames that exceed the allowed bandwidth for a particular class. Shaping, on the other hand, smooths out traffic bursts by delaying frames as needed to conform to bandwidth policies. By applying these mechanisms at Layer 2, networks can prevent individual users or applications from monopolizing switch resources and ensure fair access for all traffic classes.

CoS marking is typically performed at the point of ingress to the Layer 2 network, such as on an access switch or switch port connected to a trusted device. End-user devices such as IP phones or video conferencing systems can also apply CoS markings directly, assuming the network is configured to trust them. In this case, the switch must be configured to accept and honor the markings rather than overwrite them. In scenarios where end devices are not trusted, the switch can override CoS values based on port, VLAN, or traffic classification policies. This ensures that traffic is marked appropriately and prevents users from gaining unfair advantages by mislabeling their traffic.

Integration between Layer 2 and Layer 3 QoS mechanisms is critical for end-to-end service differentiation. CoS values can be mapped to DSCP values when traffic transitions from a Layer 2 segment into a routed segment. Conversely, when routed traffic enters a Layer 2 environment, DSCP values can be used to derive CoS markings for switch-based handling. This bidirectional mapping enables a consistent QoS policy throughout the network, from the access layer to the core and back. In MPLS networks, similar mappings exist between CoS and MPLS experimental bits, allowing for seamless traffic prioritization across different transport technologies.

Monitoring and verifying CoS behavior is an important aspect of maintaining a reliable QoS strategy. Network administrators must ensure that CoS values are being applied correctly, honored by switches, and mapped consistently across different layers. Tools such as switch port statistics, SNMP counters, and flow monitoring solutions provide visibility into traffic classes and queue utilization. These insights help detect misconfigurations, performance bottlenecks, or policy violations, allowing for timely adjustments and optimizations.

CoS plays a foundational role in delivering predictable network performance at the data link layer. While it does not offer the granularity or flexibility of higher-layer QoS mechanisms, its efficiency and speed make it indispensable in high-throughput, low-latency environments. By tagging Ethernet frames with priority information early in the transmission path, CoS ensures that important traffic is given the attention it deserves from the moment it enters the network. When used in coordination with Layer 3 QoS tools, CoS enables networks to deliver seamless, end-to-end service quality across a wide range of applications and technologies, ensuring that users experience consistent and reliable connectivity in even the most demanding scenarios.

Chapter 17: Queuing Mechanisms in Routers and Switches

Queuing mechanisms are essential components of routers and switches that determine how packets are managed when there is contention for network resources. In an ideal world, every packet arriving at a network device would be forwarded immediately without delay. However, network congestion, bandwidth limitations, and the simultaneous arrival of multiple packets create scenarios in which packets must wait in line before being transmitted. This waiting area, or queue, becomes the temporary holding space for packets until the device is ready to send them. The way packets are placed into and extracted from these queues directly influences network performance, particularly in terms of delay, jitter, packet loss, and overall Quality of Service.

At its core, a queuing mechanism must make two fundamental decisions. The first is how to categorize incoming packets. This involves determining which queue a packet should enter based on classification rules, often derived from markings such as DSCP, CoS, or IP Precedence. The second decision is how to service these queues—how frequently and in what order packets are taken from the queues and forwarded. The algorithms used to make these decisions vary widely, each with its own strengths, weaknesses, and ideal use cases. The selection and configuration of queuing mechanisms are crucial for achieving desired QoS outcomes and ensuring fairness among different traffic types.

One of the simplest queuing mechanisms is First In, First Out, or FIFO. In FIFO queuing, all packets are treated equally and processed in the order in which they arrive. This method is straightforward and efficient but lacks the ability to differentiate between traffic types. During periods of congestion, FIFO queues can become overloaded, leading to packet drops and increased latency for all traffic, regardless of importance. FIFO is most appropriate in environments where traffic is uniform and QoS is not a primary concern. However, in modern networks with diverse and competing traffic classes, more sophisticated queuing methods are necessary.

Priority Queuing is one such method that introduces a hierarchy among packets. It creates multiple queues, each assigned a different priority level. High-priority queues are serviced before lower-priority ones, ensuring that critical traffic like voice or video is forwarded with minimal delay. While this method guarantees fast service for high-priority traffic, it can starve lower-priority queues if high-priority traffic is persistent. To prevent this, network administrators must carefully monitor and manage traffic levels across all classes. Priority Queuing is highly effective for latency-sensitive applications but must be implemented with safeguards to ensure that all traffic classes receive adequate attention.

Weighted Fair Queuing, or WFQ, is a more balanced approach that addresses the limitations of both FIFO and Priority Queuing. WFQ creates separate queues for different traffic flows or classes and assigns a weight to each queue based on its relative importance. The device then services the queues in proportion to their weights, ensuring that each class receives a fair share of the bandwidth. This method provides a compromise between fairness and prioritization, making it suitable for networks that carry a mix of real-time and best-effort traffic. WFQ dynamically adapts to traffic conditions and is particularly useful in wide area networks where bandwidth is limited and must be allocated intelligently.

Class-Based Weighted Fair Queuing, or CBWFQ, extends the principles of WFQ by allowing administrators to define traffic classes explicitly and assign bandwidth percentages to each class. Unlike WFQ, which automatically identifies flows, CBWFQ uses classification policies to group traffic into logical classes. Each class has its own queue and is guaranteed a minimum share of bandwidth. This guarantees service levels for critical applications while still allowing for fair distribution among all traffic. CBWFQ is highly configurable and is often used in enterprise networks that require precise control over traffic behavior, particularly when supporting Service Level Agreements or managing multiple departments with distinct performance needs.

Low Latency Queuing, or LLQ, is an enhancement to CBWFQ that introduces strict priority scheduling for a special class of traffic. This hybrid approach allows one queue to be serviced with priority, ensuring minimal delay for real-time applications, while all other traffic is handled through CBWFQ. The priority queue is policed to prevent it from consuming all available bandwidth, thus avoiding the starvation problems associated with pure Priority Queuing. LLQ is ideal for networks that need to support voice, video, and mission-critical data simultaneously. It ensures that latency-sensitive traffic receives preferential treatment without sacrificing fairness or predictability for other traffic classes.

Another widely used mechanism is Custom Queuing, which allows administrators to define the number of bytes or packets serviced per queue in each round of scheduling. This method is less dynamic than

WFQ or CBWFQ but offers fine-grained control over service ratios. Custom Queuing can be effective in legacy systems or environments where traffic patterns are well understood and consistent. However, it lacks the flexibility and responsiveness of more modern queuing algorithms and is gradually being phased out in favor of more adaptive methods.

Random Early Detection, or RED, is not a queuing mechanism in the traditional sense but a congestion avoidance technique that works in conjunction with queues. RED monitors average queue lengths and begins dropping packets probabilistically before the queue becomes full. The goal is to signal congestion to TCP senders early, prompting them to reduce their transmission rate and thereby preventing more severe congestion and packet loss. RED can be integrated with various queuing strategies and is especially useful in environments with heavy TCP traffic. It helps maintain low delay and jitter by avoiding abrupt queue overflows and ensuring smoother traffic flow.

Queuing mechanisms are not limited to software configurations; they are also supported by hardware capabilities in modern routers and switches. High-performance devices often include dedicated memory buffers, multiple hardware queues, and specialized scheduling engines to support advanced QoS features without degrading throughput. These hardware enhancements enable queuing mechanisms to function efficiently at line speed, even in networks with gigabit or terabit data rates. The availability and configuration of queuing features can vary significantly between vendors and platforms, so careful evaluation and testing are required during network design and equipment selection.

Effective queuing is a cornerstone of QoS because it directly impacts how different types of traffic are handled under load. It enables networks to meet the performance requirements of diverse applications, from low-latency voice calls to high-throughput data transfers. The choice of queuing mechanism must align with the network's performance goals, traffic patterns, and resource constraints. Whether prioritizing real-time communication, ensuring fairness among users, or managing congestion, queuing provides the essential control needed to maintain a stable and high-performing network. With the right queuing strategies in place, organizations can confidently support a wide range of digital services while optimizing user experience and resource utilization.

Chapter 18: Priority Queuing (PQ) Explained

Priority Queuing, commonly referred to as PQ, is a foundational queuing mechanism used in network devices such as routers and switches to manage traffic based on priority levels. It is one of the earliest and simplest methods developed to address the need for Quality of Service by providing differentiated handling of network traffic. The core concept of PQ is to classify packets into discrete priority levels and always service the highest priority queue first. This ensures that critical traffic, such as voice and real-time video, receives immediate forwarding and experiences minimal delay and jitter, which are crucial for maintaining quality in real-time communications.

In a Priority Queuing system, there are typically four queues: high, medium, normal, and low. Each incoming packet is classified and placed into one of these queues based on specific criteria such as protocol type, port number, or QoS markings like DSCP or IP Precedence. The scheduling algorithm used in PQ always selects packets from the highest-priority non-empty queue, moving sequentially down to lower priorities only when higher-priority queues are empty. This strict servicing order means that as long as there is traffic in the high-priority queue, packets in the medium, normal, or low queues will not be processed.

The greatest advantage of Priority Queuing lies in its ability to guarantee low latency and jitter for time-sensitive traffic. For example, voice packets that are placed into the high-priority queue are transmitted with the utmost urgency, regardless of how congested the network may be. This makes PQ especially suitable for environments that carry real-time services over IP, such as VoIP, video conferencing, or online gaming, where delay and variability can severely impact user experience. By ensuring that these applications are never delayed behind bulk data transfers or less critical traffic, PQ helps preserve audio and video quality under varying load conditions.

However, while Priority Queuing is effective for ensuring high performance for critical traffic, it also introduces a significant risk known as starvation. Starvation occurs when lower-priority queues are never serviced because higher-priority traffic is persistent or overwhelming. In such cases, traffic in the normal or low-priority queues may be indefinitely delayed or dropped, leading to poor performance or complete disruption of non-prioritized services. This limitation makes PQ unsuitable as a standalone solution in environments with high volumes of mixed traffic. To mitigate the risk of starvation, administrators must be careful when classifying traffic and should limit the amount of data directed to the high-priority queue.

Another challenge with Priority Queuing is the lack of flexibility in bandwidth allocation. Because PQ always services higher-priority queues first, it does not provide a mechanism for distributing bandwidth equitably among different classes of traffic. This can result in inefficient use of available resources, especially when lower-priority queues are underutilized or ignored entirely. Unlike weighted queuing mechanisms, PQ does not allow for proportional sharing or bandwidth guarantees for different traffic classes. This rigidity limits its usefulness in complex network environments where a variety of applications compete for resources and where fairness is a key objective.

Despite these limitations, PQ can be highly effective when used in conjunction with other queuing mechanisms. In many modern implementations, Priority Queuing is integrated into hybrid models such as Low Latency Queuing, which combines the benefits of strict priority scheduling with the fairness of class-based weighted fair queuing. In these configurations, a single high-priority queue is reserved for delay-sensitive traffic, while remaining traffic is managed by a more balanced queuing system. This hybrid approach allows real-time applications to benefit from the responsiveness of PQ while ensuring that other traffic classes are not completely neglected.

Configuration of Priority Queuing involves several steps. First, traffic must be classified accurately to determine which packets should be placed in each priority queue. This classification can be based on Layer 3 or Layer 4 information such as IP addresses and port numbers, or on Layer 2 and Layer 3 markings like CoS or DSCP values. After classification, the PQ policy must be applied to the appropriate interface on the router or switch, ensuring that incoming packets are correctly assigned to the defined queues. Finally, it is essential to monitor traffic flows and adjust classifications as needed to prevent misuse or misconfiguration that could result in degraded performance for non-prioritized traffic.

In real-world deployments, PQ is often used in environments where a limited number of critical applications require guaranteed performance. For example, in a small office network with VoIP phones and regular data usage, PQ can be configured to prioritize voice traffic without significantly impacting file transfers or web browsing. In larger networks, PQ may be used at the edge to ensure that latency-sensitive traffic is marked and queued properly before entering the core, where more sophisticated queuing mechanisms take over. By placing real-time traffic into a high-priority queue at the earliest possible point in the network, administrators can help ensure that it receives appropriate treatment throughout its journey.

From a performance perspective, PQ is highly efficient for high-priority traffic but requires careful capacity planning and ongoing analysis to ensure that it does not cause unintended harm to other traffic types. Tools such as traffic monitoring, queue utilization statistics, and performance metrics are essential for evaluating the impact of PQ and for ensuring that the configuration continues to meet network objectives as usage patterns evolve. In addition, policy enforcement such as rate limiting or policing may be required to cap the amount of traffic eligible for high-priority treatment and to prevent abuse or accidental misclassification.

Priority Queuing remains a valuable tool in the QoS toolbox, particularly for guaranteeing performance for real-time applications. Its simplicity, predictability, and effectiveness in delivering low-latency service make it ideal for specific use cases where certain traffic must always take precedence. However, its inflexible and potentially unfair nature means that it should not be used indiscriminately or in isolation. When integrated thoughtfully into a broader QoS strategy,

PQ can play a key role in delivering a responsive and reliable user experience, supporting the demands of critical services while maintaining the overall balance and efficiency of the network.

Chapter 19: Weighted Fair Queuing (WFQ)

Weighted Fair Queuing, or WFQ, is a dynamic and intelligent queuing mechanism designed to provide fair and efficient bandwidth distribution across multiple traffic flows. It emerged as an evolution of the basic fair queuing algorithm, aiming to address the need for Quality of Service in environments where diverse applications and users compete for limited network resources. At its core, WFQ ensures that all traffic gets an appropriate share of bandwidth while still allowing higher-priority or more time-sensitive flows to receive preferential treatment when necessary. This balance between fairness and responsiveness makes WFQ particularly suitable for modern IP networks where various services, such as voice, video, file transfer, and web browsing, must coexist.

WFQ operates by creating a separate logical queue for each traffic flow. A flow is typically defined by the combination of source and destination IP address, protocol, and port numbers, although other classification methods can be used. Each flow is assigned a weight, which determines the share of bandwidth that the flow will receive relative to others. Packets are then scheduled for transmission based on these weights and their arrival times. The scheduler works to ensure that high-weight flows are serviced more frequently or with larger portions of bandwidth, while still allowing lower-weight flows to proceed in an orderly manner. This system maintains a fair allocation of resources and reduces the chances of any single flow dominating the link.

One of the strengths of WFQ lies in its ability to adapt to changing traffic conditions. Unlike static queuing mechanisms, WFQ continuously evaluates the size and timing of incoming packets to determine the best transmission order. This responsiveness is especially valuable in networks where traffic patterns are unpredictable or highly variable. WFQ dynamically adjusts queue servicing based on actual flow characteristics, preventing long flows from monopolizing the link and ensuring that short, bursty flows are not unduly delayed. This adaptability results in better performance for interactive applications and more efficient utilization of available bandwidth.

WFQ also excels at managing congestion. By allocating bandwidth proportionally and fairly, it reduces the likelihood that any single application will overwhelm the network. During periods of high traffic, WFQ can prevent latency-sensitive applications from being drowned out by bulk data transfers or other bandwidth-intensive flows. For example, in a network supporting VoIP and large file downloads, WFQ can be configured to give higher weights to voice traffic, ensuring timely delivery of voice packets while still allowing data transfers to continue, albeit at a reduced rate. This capability to control the quality and consistency of service makes WFQ a powerful tool for maintaining application performance.

In practical terms, implementing WFQ involves assigning weights either manually through administrative policies or automatically based on packet characteristics. Some WFQ systems use the IP Precedence or DSCP values in the packet header to determine the appropriate weight, integrating seamlessly with broader QoS policies. Other implementations may use predefined classes or access control lists to associate traffic with specific weights. Regardless of the method, the goal is to reflect the relative importance or performance requirements of each flow in the queuing process. Once classification and weighting are in place, the queuing system takes over, applying its scheduling algorithm to enforce fairness and efficiency.

WFQ is particularly well suited for low-speed or medium-speed interfaces, such as serial WAN links or VPN tunnels, where bandwidth must be carefully managed to prevent congestion and ensure consistent service levels. On high-speed interfaces, the number of active flows can become too large for per-flow queuing to remain efficient. In such cases, WFQ may be combined with other queuing mechanisms, such as Class-Based Weighted Fair Queuing, to aggregate flows into broader classes while still providing differentiated treatment. This scalability allows WFQ principles to be extended into more complex and demanding network environments without sacrificing control or visibility.

One of the notable features of WFQ is its fairness in handling different flow sizes. Traditional queuing mechanisms often favor large flows because they send more packets and are more likely to occupy available bandwidth. In contrast, WFQ gives equal opportunity to all flows, ensuring that small flows are not starved and that every user or application receives an appropriate level of service. This fairness is especially important in multi-tenant environments, such as shared data centers or service provider networks, where equitable treatment of customers is a key requirement. By preventing disproportionate resource consumption, WFQ helps maintain performance predictability and customer satisfaction.

WFQ also integrates well with congestion control mechanisms and network monitoring tools. Because it maintains separate queues and schedules packets based on arrival times and weights, it provides granular visibility into traffic behavior. Network administrators can observe how different flows are being serviced, identify potential bottlenecks, and fine-tune policies to improve performance. This level of insight is invaluable for capacity planning, troubleshooting, and optimizing application delivery. Moreover, when used in conjunction with traffic shaping and policing tools, WFQ becomes part of a comprehensive QoS strategy that balances throughput, delay, and fairness.

Despite its many advantages, WFQ is not without limitations. Its reliance on per-flow queuing can strain system resources, particularly in environments with a high number of simultaneous flows. The memory and processing overhead required to maintain individual queues and calculate scheduling times can become significant, especially on high-performance routers. To address this, some implementations use approximations or hybrid models that aggregate similar flows or apply simplified weighting rules. These adaptations preserve the benefits of fairness and prioritization while reducing computational demands.

Another consideration is the complexity of configuring WFQ effectively. Determining appropriate weights for different traffic types requires a deep understanding of application behavior, user needs, and network capacity. Overweighting one class can lead to underperformance in others, while misclassification can result in unfair treatment or policy violations. Successful WFQ deployment demands careful planning, ongoing monitoring, and regular adjustments to align with evolving network conditions and business priorities.

In many modern networks, WFQ serves as a building block for more advanced queuing systems. It provides the foundational logic for Class-Based Weighted Fair Queuing, which extends the concept of weighted scheduling to predefined traffic classes rather than individual flows. In this way, WFQ's principles of fairness, adaptability, and proportional service are preserved while improving scalability and manageability. Whether used alone or as part of a larger QoS architecture, WFQ remains a valuable tool for ensuring that all applications receive the network performance they require and that no single flow can dominate to the detriment of others. Its emphasis on equitable bandwidth sharing and dynamic scheduling continues to make it a preferred choice in environments where multiple services must coexist harmoniously over a shared infrastructure.

Chapter 20: Class-Based Weighted Fair Queuing (CBWFQ)

Class-Based Weighted Fair Queuing, or CBWFQ, is an advanced queuing mechanism designed to provide fine-grained control over how different classes of network traffic are treated. It is an evolution of the traditional Weighted Fair Queuing model and was developed to overcome its limitations by introducing greater administrative control and scalability. While WFQ assigns bandwidth dynamically and creates queues for individual flows, CBWFQ enables network administrators to define specific traffic classes based on business needs and allocate bandwidth explicitly to each class. This allows for predictable, consistent performance for multiple applications and services sharing a common network infrastructure, making CBWFQ an essential component of modern Quality of Service strategies.

At the core of CBWFQ is the concept of traffic classification. Instead of relying on flow-based detection, CBWFQ uses policy-based classification to group packets into classes based on criteria such as IP addresses, protocols, port numbers, or packet markings like DSCP and IP Precedence. Each class corresponds to a specific type of application or service, such as voice, video, transactional data, or best-effort traffic. Once the classification is complete, packets from each class are placed into separate queues. These queues are then serviced according to a weighted scheduling algorithm that ensures each class receives a minimum guaranteed share of the available bandwidth.

Unlike the dynamic nature of WFQ, CBWFQ requires that weights be explicitly defined by the administrator. These weights are usually configured as percentages of the total interface bandwidth or as specific bandwidth amounts in kilobits per second. For example, an organization might configure a policy where video conferencing traffic receives 30 percent of the bandwidth, voice receives 20 percent, transactional applications get 25 percent, and the remaining 25 percent is allocated to best-effort traffic. This level of control allows administrators to align network behavior with organizational priorities and application performance requirements, ensuring that critical services are always available even during periods of congestion.

A key strength of CBWFQ is its flexibility. It supports up to 64 distinct traffic classes, making it suitable for complex environments with numerous applications and usage scenarios. Each class can be configured with specific bandwidth guarantees, queuing behavior, and even packet drop policies through the use of Weighted Random Early Detection. This modularity enables highly customized QoS policies that can adapt to the specific needs of different departments, user groups, or service levels. Whether supporting a VoIP deployment in a corporate headquarters or providing tiered services in a service provider network, CBWFQ offers the precision and adaptability needed to ensure consistent service quality.

CBWFQ also supports the use of default classes. Any traffic that does not match one of the explicitly defined classes is placed into a default queue, which can be configured with its own bandwidth allocation. This ensures that all traffic is accounted for and managed, even if it falls outside the predefined policies. By avoiding a completely unclassified best-effort queue, CBWFQ maintains control over all data on the interface, reducing the risk of unexpected congestion or performance degradation.

One of the primary use cases for CBWFQ is in enterprise networks that support multiple mission-critical applications over a single WAN link. In such environments, different applications have varying sensitivities to delay, jitter, and loss. CBWFQ allows administrators to guarantee the necessary resources for delay-sensitive traffic like voice and video, while still allocating sufficient bandwidth for data applications. This predictable and proportional distribution of resources improves the overall efficiency of the network and ensures a high-quality experience for all users.

When implementing CBWFQ, it is crucial to understand the characteristics and requirements of the traffic on the network. Traffic analysis tools, historical usage data, and performance benchmarks can help identify the appropriate classes and determine how much bandwidth each class requires. Over-provisioning a class can lead to underutilization of resources, while under-provisioning can cause performance issues and user dissatisfaction. CBWFQ configurations should be revisited periodically to account for changes in traffic patterns, application behavior, or business priorities.

Another important aspect of CBWFQ is how it interacts with congestion and packet loss. During times of congestion, if a class exceeds its allocated bandwidth, packets may be queued or dropped depending on the configuration. By integrating CBWFQ with WRED, administrators can control how packets are dropped within each class. WRED uses statistical thresholds to drop packets early in an intelligent manner, preventing global synchronization and reducing the likelihood of buffer overflow. This helps maintain throughput while minimizing the impact of congestion on application performance.

While CBWFQ offers powerful capabilities, it also introduces complexity. Defining multiple classes, configuring bandwidth allocations, and monitoring performance require a deep understanding of network behavior and QoS principles. Improperly configured policies can lead to inefficient use of bandwidth, unfair treatment of traffic, or even outages. To ensure effective implementation, it is recommended to follow a structured approach that includes traffic profiling, policy design, simulation or testing, and continuous monitoring.

CBWFQ also integrates well with other QoS mechanisms. For instance, when combined with traffic shaping, it can help smooth traffic bursts and ensure that bandwidth limits are respected over time. With policing, it can enforce maximum rates for certain classes, dropping or remarking packets that exceed policy limits. When used in conjunction with Low Latency Queuing, CBWFQ can support a special priority class for delay-sensitive traffic while maintaining weighted fair queuing for all other classes. This integration makes CBWFQ a cornerstone of comprehensive QoS strategies across a wide range of network topologies and service models.

In summary, Class-Based Weighted Fair Queuing brings structure, predictability, and fairness to network traffic management. Its policy-based approach to classification and bandwidth allocation empowers administrators to implement granular QoS strategies tailored to specific business requirements. By enabling multiple traffic classes to coexist and receive guaranteed service levels, CBWFQ plays a critical role in optimizing network performance, supporting real-time applications, and ensuring that user experience remains consistent and reliable. As networks continue to support more diverse and demanding applications, the role of CBWFQ in maintaining service quality and operational efficiency becomes increasingly vital.

Chapter 21: Low Latency Queuing (LLQ)

Low Latency Queuing, commonly abbreviated as LLQ, is an advanced queuing mechanism designed to deliver superior Quality of Service by combining the strengths of both priority queuing and class-based weighted fair queuing. It was introduced to overcome the limitations of individual queuing models, particularly in scenarios where real-time applications must coexist with bulk data transfers and other routine network services. LLQ addresses the critical need for prioritization of delay-sensitive traffic while maintaining fair and predictable treatment for all other types of traffic. It is especially effective in environments where voice, video, and other interactive applications share the same network paths as transactional and best-effort data.

The core idea behind LLQ is to integrate a strict priority queue within the framework of class-based weighted fair queuing. This integration allows one specific class of traffic to receive priority handling, meaning its packets are sent before any others as long as they are present in the queue. This priority class is typically reserved for traffic types that are extremely sensitive to delay and jitter, such as Voice over IP (VoIP) or real-time video streams. By isolating this traffic into a dedicated priority queue, LLQ ensures that these packets experience minimal delay and are forwarded immediately upon arrival, provided that the link is not already transmitting another packet.

Unlike traditional priority queuing, which could lead to the starvation of lower-priority traffic when high-priority flows are continuous, LLQ incorporates policing mechanisms that cap the amount of bandwidth the priority class can consume. This prevents it from monopolizing the link and ensures that other traffic classes, managed by class-based weighted fair queuing, still receive their configured shares of bandwidth. This combination achieves a balance between responsiveness for real-time traffic and fairness for all other applications. It provides a practical solution for networks where maintaining voice quality is just as important as ensuring reliable access to cloud applications, web services, and file transfers.

In LLQ, traffic classification is essential. Packets are first analyzed and assigned to classes based on characteristics such as IP address, port number, or QoS markings like DSCP. One class, and only one, can be designated as the priority class. This class is mapped to the strict priority queue. The remaining traffic is assigned to other classes and managed using the CBWFQ framework, which allocates bandwidth based on configured weights. These weights define the minimum bandwidth guarantees for each class, ensuring that even during congestion, essential services receive a consistent level of performance. This multi-class approach provides the flexibility needed to tailor QoS policies to the specific needs of different applications and users.

The priority queue in LLQ is serviced with absolute precedence over all other queues. This means that when packets exist in the priority queue, they are transmitted before any other packet, regardless of class or weight. To prevent abuse and ensure system stability, LLQ enforces a bandwidth limit on the priority class, often configured as a percentage of the total link bandwidth or as a specific kilobits-per-second value. If the priority traffic exceeds this limit, excess packets may be dropped or delayed according to policy. This policing mechanism is crucial because it maintains fairness while still providing the low-latency service that real-time applications require.

One of the most common use cases for LLQ is in networks that support Voice over IP. VoIP traffic is highly sensitive to both delay and jitter, and even small variances in packet arrival times can result in noticeable degradation in audio quality. By placing voice packets into the LLQ priority queue, network administrators can ensure that voice communications remain clear and reliable, even when the network is under heavy load. Similarly, LLQ is beneficial for real-time video applications such as telepresence or video conferencing, where delays or frame loss can disrupt user experience. With LLQ, these applications can maintain their quality without being impacted by large file transfers or background data synchronization.

LLQ can also be used to support other critical services that require immediate forwarding. For example, control-plane traffic in industrial networks, signaling messages in financial trading systems, or emergency alerts in public safety networks can all benefit from the guaranteed low-latency treatment that LLQ provides. However, it is important to use the priority queue sparingly. Only the most essential traffic should be assigned to it, as excessive use can lead to policing penalties and unintended packet drops. Misclassifying traffic into the priority queue not only degrades service for other classes but may also result in inconsistent behavior for the supposed high-priority flows themselves.

Implementing LLQ effectively requires a thorough understanding of the network's traffic patterns and application requirements. Administrators must analyze usage data, identify which services are delay-sensitive, and configure classification policies accordingly. LLQ must be applied at appropriate points in the network, typically on WAN interfaces or other bandwidth-constrained links where congestion is likely to occur. It is also important to coordinate LLQ policies across multiple devices to ensure consistent end-to-end treatment of priority traffic. Inconsistent configurations can lead to bottlenecks or packet reordering, negating the benefits of the mechanism.

Monitoring and adjusting LLQ configurations is an ongoing process. Tools such as SNMP counters, queuing statistics, and real-time traffic monitors help administrators assess the performance of each class, detect congestion, and verify that bandwidth allocations are being respected. If priority traffic begins to exceed its configured limit, administrators may need to increase the allocation or optimize application behavior to reduce bandwidth demands. At the same time, ensuring that non-priority traffic maintains acceptable performance may require adjusting weights in the CBWFQ classes or implementing additional shaping and policing strategies.

The success of LLQ depends on disciplined and thoughtful application. When configured correctly, it delivers excellent performance for real-time applications without sacrificing service quality for other traffic types. It provides a structured and scalable way to ensure that critical communications always receive the network resources they need, even in the most demanding conditions. LLQ represents the convergence of two powerful queuing philosophies: the precision of strict priority scheduling and the fairness of class-based weighted distribution. This hybrid design allows organizations to meet stringent service-level requirements while preserving the integrity and performance of their overall network infrastructure. As the need for high-performance, converged networks continues to grow, LLQ remains a cornerstone technique for delivering reliable and differentiated Quality of Service across a wide range of environments.

Chapter 22: Policing vs. Shaping

Policing and shaping are two fundamental traffic control techniques used in Quality of Service to regulate the flow of data through a network. While both serve the purpose of enforcing traffic policies and managing bandwidth usage, they operate in different ways and are suited to different scenarios. Understanding the differences between these two mechanisms is critical for designing networks that can maintain performance, ensure fairness, and avoid congestion, particularly when supporting a wide variety of applications with diverse requirements. Each method has its strengths and trade-offs, and choosing the appropriate one depends on the desired outcome, the network architecture, and the characteristics of the traffic being managed.

Policing is a method of traffic control that monitors the rate at which packets arrive on an interface or within a flow and enforces a strict limit on that rate. If traffic exceeds the configured threshold, the excess packets are either dropped immediately or marked for possible downstream discard. The process of marking typically involves changing a field in the packet header, such as the Differentiated Services Code Point or IP Precedence, so that subsequent devices in the path can treat the packet as lower priority. Policing is a reactive mechanism; it does not buffer or delay excess packets but rather takes immediate action based on current conditions. It is often used to enforce service level agreements, prevent abuse of bandwidth policies, and ensure that traffic conforms to expected profiles.

Shaping, on the other hand, is a proactive approach that delays packets to control the flow rate. Instead of dropping packets that exceed a configured rate, a traffic shaper temporarily stores the excess packets in a buffer and releases them at a consistent, pre-defined rate. This smooths out bursts and ensures a more predictable traffic pattern, which is especially important in avoiding congestion on downstream links. Shaping introduces controlled latency but preserves packet delivery, making it suitable for traffic types that can tolerate some delay but not loss. It is commonly used on interfaces that connect to lower-speed links or networks with strict rate expectations, such as wide area network connections or interfaces with metered bandwidth.

The key operational difference between policing and shaping lies in how they treat excess traffic. Policing is stricter, enforcing hard limits by either discarding or reclassifying packets, whereas shaping is more lenient, smoothing traffic to fit within the desired parameters. Because policing does not buffer packets, it can result in packet loss and reordering, which may negatively impact certain applications, particularly those that rely on consistent delivery, such as voice and video. Shaping, by contrast, preserves packet order and delivery at the cost of added delay, which can be acceptable for many types of data traffic.

Another important distinction is that shaping requires the presence of a queue or buffer to store excess packets, while policing does not. This means that shaping requires more memory and processing resources, and may introduce jitter if the buffer becomes too full. However, the benefits of smoothing traffic and preventing bursts from overwhelming the network often outweigh these drawbacks, particularly when managing large data transfers or interacting with external networks that have strict rate expectations. In some implementations, shaping also includes the use of tokens or leaky bucket algorithms to calculate how much data can be transmitted at any given moment, allowing for precise control of traffic flow over time.

Policing is generally used at network ingress points, where it serves as the first line of defense against traffic that exceeds acceptable levels. This might include customer-facing interfaces in a service provider network, where traffic must be limited according to contractual terms, or at the edge of a corporate network, where internal traffic must conform to policy. By immediately discarding or remarking traffic that violates rules, policing protects internal resources and prevents misbehaving flows from affecting other users. It is also useful in enforcing per-user or per-application limits, ensuring that no single entity can monopolize shared bandwidth.

Shaping, by contrast, is more commonly deployed at network egress points, particularly before sending traffic onto a link with a lower capacity than the internal network. For example, a high-speed core network may deliver traffic to a slower WAN link, where shaping is used to match the rate of traffic to the capacity of the outbound link. Without shaping, bursts of traffic from the high-speed network could cause congestion and packet loss at the WAN interface. By buffering and pacing the traffic, shaping allows for a more controlled transition and minimizes the risk of loss. This approach is particularly valuable for maintaining service quality and avoiding retransmissions, which can further burden constrained links.

There are scenarios where both policing and shaping are used together in a coordinated fashion. For example, traffic may be shaped to a target rate and then policed to ensure compliance. Alternatively, different classes of traffic may be subject to different treatments, with real-time traffic being shaped to maintain consistent delay while background traffic is policed to prevent excessive usage. This layered approach allows for a more nuanced and effective QoS strategy, aligning the treatment of traffic with its specific performance needs and the capabilities of the network infrastructure.

Each method also has implications for compliance and monitoring. Policing provides a clear-cut mechanism for enforcing limits, making it easier to detect violations and enforce accountability. Shaping, while more forgiving, requires more sophisticated monitoring to assess buffer behavior and measure latency impacts. Tools such as SNMP, NetFlow, and advanced traffic analytics are essential for understanding the performance of policing and shaping policies and for making informed adjustments to maintain service quality.

In real-world networks, the choice between policing and shaping is not always binary. Instead, it involves careful consideration of application requirements, network architecture, and operational goals. For instance, in a voice network, shaping might be preferred to ensure smooth audio delivery, while in a data center, policing might be used to enforce strict limits on tenant traffic. The effectiveness of either method depends on accurate traffic classification, thoughtful configuration, and continuous performance evaluation.

Policing and shaping represent two sides of the same coin in traffic management. One enforces rules with precision and immediacy, the other with patience and control. Each serves a distinct purpose, and when used wisely, they provide the network with the tools to deliver fairness, efficiency, and high-quality service across a diverse range of applications and users. As networks continue to grow in complexity and demand, these mechanisms will remain essential to achieving consistent and predictable behavior in a dynamic and data-intensive environment.

Chapter 23: Traffic Policing Techniques

Traffic policing techniques are critical components in the implementation of Quality of Service in IP networks. They serve as enforcement tools that regulate the amount of traffic entering or traversing a network by monitoring traffic rates and applying specific actions when traffic exceeds predefined thresholds. Unlike shaping, which smooths traffic by buffering excess packets, policing is a more immediate method that either drops or re-marks packets that do not conform to the configured rate. This aggressive approach makes policing particularly useful in enforcing service level agreements, protecting shared resources, and maintaining fairness in environments where multiple users or services compete for bandwidth.

The most basic function of a traffic policer is to measure the rate at which packets arrive and compare it to a configured rate limit. If the traffic rate remains within the acceptable range, packets are forwarded normally. If the rate is exceeded, the policer can take one of several actions. The most common actions include dropping the offending packets or re-marking them with a lower priority. Re-marking involves altering specific fields in the packet header, such as the Differentiated Services Code Point or IP Precedence, to signal that the packet should receive less favorable treatment downstream. This approach allows the network to continue carrying excess traffic but without guaranteeing performance, as it may be discarded if congestion occurs further along the path.

Policing mechanisms typically rely on token-based algorithms to determine compliance. One widely used method is the single-rate, two-color marker, which monitors traffic against a single committed information rate. In this model, packets are classified as either conforming or exceeding based on whether they fall within the configured rate. If the rate is exceeded, excess packets are either dropped or re-marked. This simple model is effective for basic rate limiting, but it lacks the flexibility to accommodate variable traffic patterns or provide multiple levels of treatment for excess traffic.

To address this, more advanced policing techniques use the single-rate, three-color marker or the two-rate, three-color marker. In the single-rate, three-color model, traffic is classified into three categories:

conforming, exceeding, and violating. This model introduces a committed burst size in addition to the committed information rate, allowing for temporary bursts of traffic to be tolerated without penalty. Packets that fall within the committed rate and burst size are marked as conforming. Those that exceed the committed rate but fall within an allowable burst are marked as exceeding, while packets beyond both limits are marked as violating and typically dropped.

The two-rate, three-color marker introduces even greater granularity by incorporating two rate parameters: a committed information rate and a peak information rate. This model allows network administrators to define not only how much bandwidth a flow should receive under normal conditions but also how much can be tolerated under peak usage. Packets are again classified into three categories. Conforming packets meet the committed rate, exceeding packets are within the peak rate but above the committed rate, and violating packets exceed both thresholds. This approach enables more flexible policies that differentiate between acceptable excess traffic and abusive traffic, providing a more nuanced control over how resources are allocated and protected.

In addition to rate measurement and packet marking, traffic policing techniques also include mechanisms for integrating with other QoS tools such as access control lists, class-based classification, and congestion management. For instance, a policy might use access control lists to identify traffic from a specific source and then apply a policing action that limits the rate to a specified threshold. If the traffic exceeds that rate, packets might be re-marked with a lower DSCP value, ensuring that they are deprioritized by downstream devices. These combined policies allow network administrators to implement sophisticated controls that align with business objectives, user needs, and technical constraints.

Policing can be applied at various points in the network. At the edge, it is often used to limit incoming traffic from external sources or user devices, ensuring that only compliant traffic enters the network. This is particularly important in multi-tenant environments or service provider networks, where customers must be isolated and limited according to their contractual bandwidth. Within the core, policing can be used to enforce policies between internal departments or to prevent specific applications from consuming excessive resources. On outbound interfaces, policing ensures that traffic sent to external networks complies with externally defined rate limits or service agreements.

One of the challenges of policing is its impact on sensitive applications. Because policing drops or re-marks packets without buffering, it can introduce loss, reordering, or inconsistent service levels, especially for real-time applications such as voice and video. These applications are highly sensitive to jitter and loss, and even a small percentage of dropped packets can lead to noticeable degradation in quality. For this reason, traffic policing must be configured carefully and should not be applied indiscriminately to all types of traffic. In environments where real-time performance is essential, alternative techniques such as traffic shaping or low latency queuing may be more appropriate.

Monitoring and analyzing the effects of policing is an essential part of effective QoS management. Modern network devices provide extensive statistics on policy performance, including the number of packets that have been dropped, re-marked, or forwarded under each policing rule. These statistics help administrators verify that policies are working as intended and allow for adjustments based on observed behavior. For example, if a policing rule is dropping an unexpected volume of traffic, the rate or burst size might need to be increased. Conversely, if a user or application is consistently exceeding limits, more stringent policing may be required to maintain fairness and protect other traffic.

As networks continue to grow in scale and complexity, the importance of traffic policing remains significant. With the rise of cloud services, mobile applications, and high-bandwidth media, the potential for congestion and unfair resource usage is greater than ever. Policing provides a simple yet powerful tool to enforce order and predictability in such environments. By setting clear boundaries and acting on violations, it ensures that network resources are used efficiently and equitably. When combined with other QoS mechanisms, traffic policing helps deliver a consistent and high-quality experience to all users, regardless of network conditions or usage demands. Whether applied to prevent abuse, enforce contracts, or shape application behavior, policing remains an indispensable part of traffic management in modern IP networks.

Chapter 24: Traffic Shaping Methods

Traffic shaping is a crucial technique in network management that involves regulating the flow of data to conform to a specified rate. Unlike policing, which drops or marks excess packets, shaping delays them by buffering and releasing them gradually to smooth out bursts. This method is particularly effective in managing congestion, optimizing bandwidth utilization, and ensuring the consistent delivery of packets across varying network conditions. Traffic shaping is proactive and preserves packet integrity, making it an ideal choice for many enterprise and service provider environments where packet loss and reordering can degrade performance.

At the heart of traffic shaping is the concept of rate control. Traffic shaping operates by enforcing a sustained output rate, which is usually defined in bits per second. When the amount of incoming data exceeds this rate, the shaping mechanism holds packets in a buffer and schedules their transmission at intervals that maintain the configured throughput. This helps avoid sudden surges of traffic that could overwhelm downstream devices or links. By introducing controlled latency rather than discarding packets, shaping maintains the fidelity of communication, making it suitable for applications that are sensitive to loss but tolerant to delay.

One of the most common traffic shaping methods is the token bucket algorithm. This algorithm controls the amount of data that can be transmitted based on the accumulation of tokens in a bucket. Tokens are generated at a fixed rate, and each token allows a certain amount of data, typically a byte or packet, to be sent. When data arrives, it can only be transmitted if enough tokens are available. If there are not enough tokens, the data is buffered until sufficient tokens accumulate. This approach allows for bursts of traffic up to a defined burst size while still maintaining an average transmission rate over time. It strikes a balance between flexibility and control, making it one of the most widely used algorithms in traffic shaping implementations.

Another method often associated with shaping is the leaky bucket algorithm. This method enforces a strict output rate, where packets leak out of the bucket at a steady rate, much like water dripping from a hole. Any incoming packets that exceed the bucket's capacity are held in the buffer and released at the configured rate. The leaky bucket algorithm is more rigid than the token bucket, providing consistent spacing between packets and preventing large bursts. It is particularly useful in environments where deterministic behavior is required, such as in financial systems or industrial networks where timing precision is critical.

In practice, traffic shaping is applied at various points within a network. It is commonly used on outbound interfaces, especially when transmitting traffic to a lower-speed link or an external network with known bandwidth limitations. By shaping traffic before it exits the network, administrators can prevent packet loss that would occur if bursts were sent to a link that cannot handle them. This is especially relevant in enterprise WAN links, where shaping can be used to match the transmission rate to the capabilities of the service provider's network. In such scenarios, shaping ensures compliance with service level agreements and avoids triggering congestion on upstream infrastructure.

Traffic shaping can also be used internally within a network to manage flows between different segments or departments. For example, in a campus network where departments share a common backbone, shaping can ensure that no single group consumes disproportionate bandwidth during peak periods. By applying shaping policies based on traffic classes or user identities, organizations can enforce fair usage policies and maintain service quality for all users. This internal shaping is often integrated with access control and quality of service policies to create a cohesive network management strategy.

One of the advantages of traffic shaping is its ability to work in tandem with other QoS mechanisms such as queuing, scheduling, and congestion avoidance. For instance, shaped traffic can be passed through class-based weighted fair queuing to ensure that each class receives its fair share of bandwidth after rate control has been applied. Additionally, shaping can be combined with marking strategies, where packets are tagged with DSCP values as they are shaped, indicating their priority to downstream devices. This coordination between shaping and QoS classification allows for end-to-end service consistency, particularly in multi-hop environments or across provider boundaries.

Advanced shaping implementations allow for hierarchical shaping, where traffic is shaped at multiple levels. For example, an interface may apply an overall shaping policy while also enforcing shaping rules for individual traffic classes within that interface. This nested approach allows for granular control over bandwidth usage and is particularly useful in complex network environments with a wide range of services and performance requirements. Hierarchical shaping is commonly seen in service provider networks and large enterprise deployments where multiple tenants or service types share the same physical infrastructure.

Monitoring the effectiveness of traffic shaping is essential for maintaining network performance and meeting operational goals. Network administrators rely on statistics such as queue depth, buffer utilization, dropped packet counts, and throughput measurements to evaluate shaping performance. These metrics provide insights into whether shaping policies are achieving their intended results or if adjustments are needed. For instance, consistently full buffers may indicate that the shaping rate is too low, leading to increased latency. On the other hand, underutilized buffers might suggest that the shaping policy is too conservative and that bandwidth could be allocated more aggressively.

Traffic shaping can also be adaptive. Some modern implementations allow shaping rates to be adjusted dynamically based on real-time network conditions or application requirements. This flexibility enables the network to respond to changes in demand, providing more bandwidth to applications when resources are available and tightening control during congestion. Adaptive shaping is particularly beneficial in cloud environments or software-defined networks, where traffic patterns can be unpredictable and demand rapid, automated responses from the infrastructure.

Implementing traffic shaping effectively requires a thorough understanding of network topology, traffic behavior, and application performance needs. Shaping policies must be carefully designed to match actual usage patterns, taking into account peak loads, burst characteristics, and latency sensitivity. Misconfigured shaping can introduce excessive delay, create bottlenecks, or even starve critical applications of needed bandwidth. Therefore, ongoing analysis, performance testing, and policy refinement are essential to maintaining a healthy network that leverages shaping to its fullest potential.

Traffic shaping is a vital tool for achieving controlled and consistent data transmission across networks of all sizes. Its ability to smooth traffic flows, prevent congestion, and prioritize applications without dropping packets makes it indispensable in modern QoS strategies. By introducing order into potentially chaotic traffic patterns, shaping empowers networks to support diverse applications while delivering a high-quality experience to users. As demand for real-time, high-throughput, and latency-sensitive services continues to grow, shaping will remain a central mechanism for managing network behavior and ensuring optimal resource utilization.

Chapter 25: Token Bucket and Leaky Bucket Algorithms

The Token Bucket and Leaky Bucket algorithms are two fundamental models used in traffic management for enforcing bandwidth limitations, controlling congestion, and ensuring compliance with Quality of Service policies in IP networks. Both mechanisms provide the ability to regulate data flow rates and are frequently applied in shaping and policing configurations. While they are often used in similar contexts, these algorithms differ in how they handle traffic bursts, manage buffers, and control packet transmission. Understanding how each algorithm operates is essential for designing effective QoS strategies and for selecting the appropriate method depending on application requirements and network behavior.

The Token Bucket algorithm is designed to allow short bursts of data transmission while still enforcing a long-term average rate. It works by generating tokens at a steady rate and placing them in a logical container known as the bucket. Each token typically represents the right to send a unit of data, such as one byte or one packet. When a packet arrives, it must capture a number of tokens equal to its size in order to be transmitted. If enough tokens are available, the packet is forwarded immediately. If not, the packet must either wait in a buffer until enough tokens accumulate or be discarded, depending on the specific implementation and configuration of the traffic management system.

One of the strengths of the Token Bucket algorithm is its burst-tolerant behavior. When the network is idle or underutilized, tokens continue to accumulate in the bucket up to a defined maximum known as the burst size. This stored capacity allows for sudden increases in data transmission when needed. For example, if a user initiates a large file transfer after a period of inactivity, the accumulated tokens can be used to transmit data at a rate that temporarily exceeds the average. This capability makes the Token Bucket algorithm ideal for applications that generate intermittent traffic but require high throughput when they are active. It allows for flexibility without compromising the enforcement of long-term bandwidth contracts.

In contrast, the Leaky Bucket algorithm enforces a more rigid and uniform flow of data. It is conceptually similar to a bucket with a small hole at the bottom, through which data leaks out at a constant rate. When a packet arrives, it is placed in the bucket if there is space available. The bucket has a fixed size, and packets are removed and transmitted at a steady, predefined rate. If the bucket is full when a packet arrives, the packet is dropped immediately. This approach provides strict control over output rate and is effective in smoothing traffic and eliminating bursts entirely. It ensures a consistent and predictable data flow, which is advantageous in scenarios where timing and pacing are critical.

The Leaky Bucket algorithm is less tolerant of traffic bursts because it does not allow for the accumulation of transmission credits like the Token Bucket does. Its primary strength is in shaping traffic to conform to a fixed output rate, regardless of how the data arrives. This makes it useful for applications that demand highly regulated transmission or for networks where bursty traffic could cause buffer overflows or service degradation. By limiting the data rate and smoothing traffic at the source, the Leaky Bucket helps prevent downstream congestion and improves the reliability of time-sensitive services.

Despite their differences, both algorithms share common goals in managing network resources and maintaining service quality. They provide mechanisms to ensure that traffic conforms to pre-established bandwidth limitations, helping to enforce service level agreements and prevent network abuse. When implemented as part of a broader QoS policy, these algorithms can work alongside classification, queuing, and marking techniques to provide comprehensive traffic control and prioritization. For instance, shaped traffic using a Token Bucket may be marked with a higher priority than traffic that is policed with a Leaky Bucket, reflecting the difference in treatment and tolerance for deviation.

In modern networking environments, the choice between Token Bucket and Leaky Bucket is often determined by the nature of the traffic and the objectives of the policy being enforced. For example, a Token Bucket might be chosen for voice traffic that occasionally requires bursts to maintain call quality, while a Leaky Bucket might be applied to transactional systems where consistent delivery intervals are more important than speed. Some implementations even combine the two algorithms to provide enhanced flexibility. In such hybrid configurations, a Leaky Bucket may be used to shape the output of a Token Bucket, ensuring that bursts are permitted but also paced carefully to prevent downstream issues.

Another consideration is how these algorithms are implemented in hardware or software. In high-performance routers and switches, traffic shaping and policing mechanisms are often accelerated by dedicated hardware, which must support fast and accurate rate calculation. Efficient implementation of the Token Bucket algorithm involves maintaining a running count of available tokens, recalculating token generation over time, and updating the count each time a packet is transmitted. Similarly, Leaky Bucket implementations must manage a queue, ensure consistent interval transmission, and detect overflow conditions rapidly. Performance, scalability, and precision are all critical factors in making these algorithms viable at the scale required by modern networks.

Monitoring and tuning these algorithms is also vital for ensuring they meet performance expectations. Administrators must configure parameters such as committed information rate, burst size, bucket depth, and maximum transmission unit with care. Misconfiguration can result in unintended packet loss, excessive delay, or inefficient bandwidth usage. For example, setting the token generation rate too low may throttle traffic unnecessarily, while an overly large burst size might cause unexpected spikes that overwhelm downstream systems. By continuously analyzing traffic patterns and adjusting parameters accordingly, network engineers can optimize the behavior of both Token Bucket and Leaky Bucket algorithms to align with business and application goals.

Both Token Bucket and Leaky Bucket algorithms play an indispensable role in network traffic management. Their distinct characteristics and operational models provide network designers with flexible tools to meet a wide range of service requirements. Whether used for enforcing bandwidth limits, shaping traffic for consistency, or policing flows to prevent congestion, these algorithms contribute significantly to the overall stability and performance of the network. As digital services become more demanding and users expect consistent, high-quality experiences, the importance of precise and efficient traffic control mechanisms will only grow, solidifying the role of Token Bucket and Leaky Bucket as foundational components in modern Quality of Service architectures.

Chapter 26: Bandwidth Allocation Strategies

Bandwidth allocation strategies are essential for managing the finite capacity of network resources in a way that aligns with organizational priorities, application demands, and user expectations. In modern IP networks, where a wide range of applications operate simultaneously and often compete for access to the same transmission paths, the ability to allocate bandwidth efficiently is a cornerstone of effective Quality of Service implementation. Proper bandwidth allocation ensures that critical services receive the necessary throughput, while non-essential traffic is either limited or delayed in accordance with its relative importance. The ultimate goal is to maximize performance and user experience while avoiding congestion, bottlenecks, and unfair resource distribution.

One of the most fundamental approaches to bandwidth allocation is static provisioning. In this model, administrators assign fixed portions of available bandwidth to specific applications, user groups, or traffic classes based on known usage patterns and business requirements. For example, voice traffic may be allocated 20 percent of the link capacity, video 30 percent, and the remaining 50 percent reserved for data and best-effort services. Static provisioning is straightforward and predictable, allowing for clear expectations and consistent service levels. However, it lacks flexibility and can result in underutilization when assigned bandwidth is not fully consumed, or in performance degradation when an application temporarily needs more capacity than it has been allotted.

To address the limitations of static models, many networks implement dynamic bandwidth allocation strategies. These strategies rely on real-time traffic analysis and automated decision-making to adjust allocations based on current conditions. One example is demand-based allocation, where bandwidth is distributed according to the actual needs of applications at any given moment. If video conferencing traffic increases during a specific period, the network can temporarily assign more bandwidth to that class while reducing capacity for less active services. This elasticity improves efficiency and responsiveness, ensuring that applications receive the resources they require when they need them most.

Another widely used method is priority-based bandwidth allocation. In this approach, traffic is classified into hierarchical levels of importance, and bandwidth is allocated preferentially to higher-priority classes. For instance, mission-critical applications such as VoIP or enterprise resource planning systems are granted immediate access to bandwidth, while background tasks such as file downloads or software updates are assigned lower priority and may experience delays during congestion. Priority-based allocation is often implemented using queuing mechanisms like Low Latency Queuing or Class-Based Weighted Fair Queuing, which not only differentiate traffic but also manage how bandwidth is shared across classes. This method ensures that delay-sensitive applications maintain consistent performance regardless of network load.

Weighted allocation is a related strategy that provides a more granular level of control by assigning weights to different traffic classes. Each class receives a portion of bandwidth in proportion to its assigned weight, allowing for equitable and customizable distribution. Unlike strict priority models, weighted allocation avoids starvation of lower-priority traffic by guaranteeing minimum service levels for all classes. This is particularly useful in networks that must support a diverse range of applications with varying performance expectations. Weighted allocation supports fairness while still enabling prioritization, making it a popular choice for enterprise and service provider environments alike.

In shared network environments, such as broadband access or multi-tenant data centers, bandwidth allocation strategies must also account for user isolation and fairness. Fair queuing techniques such as Weighted Fair Queuing ensure that no single user or application can monopolize the link, promoting equitable access for all participants. These methods create virtual queues for each flow or user and distribute bandwidth proportionally based on predefined policies. This is essential for maintaining a consistent quality of experience, especially in public or commercial networks where customers expect predictable performance despite variable demand.

Time-based bandwidth allocation is another strategic approach used in networks with predictable usage cycles. By analyzing historical data, administrators can identify patterns in traffic demand and configure policies that adjust bandwidth availability during specific time windows. For example, more bandwidth can be allocated to online collaboration tools during business hours and reallocated to backup operations overnight. This type of time-aware strategy maximizes efficiency and aligns resource usage with actual needs. It also supports policy enforcement aligned with organizational schedules or service level agreements.

Application-aware bandwidth allocation introduces even greater sophistication by integrating deep packet inspection or behavioral analytics into the allocation process. By identifying specific applications within traffic flows, the network can apply tailored bandwidth policies that reflect the unique requirements of each application. For instance, streaming services may be limited to a certain bandwidth ceiling to prevent congestion, while real-time control systems receive unrestricted access due to their sensitivity to delay. Application awareness enables precise control, reducing the risk of over-provisioning and ensuring that performance-critical services remain unaffected by bandwidth-intensive but non-essential traffic.

In cloud and virtualized environments, bandwidth allocation becomes even more dynamic. Virtual machines and containers often spin up and down rapidly, generating variable traffic loads across shared infrastructure. Network function virtualization and software-defined networking technologies provide the programmability and visibility needed to allocate bandwidth dynamically based on real-time demand and policy definitions. By abstracting bandwidth control from physical interfaces and embedding it into virtual overlays, these environments can enforce consistent allocation strategies at scale. Automated orchestration tools can monitor application performance and adjust bandwidth allocations continuously, ensuring optimal usage of available resources.

One of the most challenging aspects of bandwidth allocation is striking the right balance between efficiency and fairness. Allocating too much bandwidth to a single application or user can lead to congestion for others, while overly rigid controls may prevent legitimate bursts or fail to accommodate growing demand. Therefore, effective bandwidth allocation strategies require constant monitoring, analysis, and adjustment. Performance metrics such as throughput, latency, packet loss, and utilization must be collected and evaluated to determine whether current policies are meeting their objectives. When deviations are detected, policies must be refined to align with evolving traffic patterns and business needs.

Bandwidth allocation is not only a technical necessity but also a strategic enabler for digital transformation. As organizations adopt more cloud services, support remote workforces, and expand into digital services, the need for intelligent and responsive bandwidth management becomes increasingly critical. Bandwidth must be treated as a valuable and finite asset that must be allocated in a way that supports strategic priorities while preserving operational stability. The right allocation strategy can enhance application performance, improve user satisfaction, reduce operational costs, and ensure compliance with regulatory or contractual obligations. Whether through static assignments, dynamic adjustments, or hybrid models, bandwidth allocation will remain a core pillar of network design and QoS engineering in the years ahead.

Chapter 27: QoS in WAN Environments

Quality of Service in Wide Area Network environments plays a pivotal role in ensuring reliable and consistent communication across geographically dispersed locations. Unlike local area networks, which typically benefit from high bandwidth, low latency, and minimal congestion, WAN environments are often characterized by constrained bandwidth, variable delays, and higher levels of traffic unpredictability. These conditions make QoS mechanisms not only desirable but essential for maintaining the performance and availability of critical applications that rely on WAN connectivity. Organizations increasingly depend on WANs to connect branch offices, remote users, data centers, and cloud services, and as such, QoS must be implemented thoughtfully to overcome the inherent limitations of wide-area transmission.

The unique characteristics of WAN links pose specific challenges for QoS. Bandwidth on WAN circuits is typically more expensive and limited compared to internal LAN segments, which makes efficient use of available capacity a top priority. High latency and potential packet loss can degrade performance for real-time applications such as voice and video conferencing, which are sensitive to jitter and delay. Moreover, WAN traffic often traverses service provider networks, where administrative control is shared or limited, introducing complexity in applying and enforcing QoS policies consistently from end to end.

To effectively implement QoS in a WAN environment, traffic must be classified and marked as close to the source as possible, often at the edge router or customer-premises equipment. This classification process identifies the type of traffic—whether it is voice, video, transactional data, or best-effort traffic—and marks it using mechanisms such as DSCP values. These markings inform subsequent network devices about how each packet should be treated. In the WAN context, it is critical that service providers honor these markings or provide mapping between customer-defined classes and their internal QoS policies. This cooperation is usually formalized in service-level agreements, which specify how many classes of service are supported and how bandwidth is allocated among them.

One of the most commonly applied QoS techniques in WANs is traffic shaping. By regulating the flow of outgoing traffic to match the contractual rate with the service provider, shaping helps prevent congestion and packet loss at the provider's edge. This is particularly important when an organization's internal network operates at a higher speed than the WAN link. Traffic shaping smooths out bursts and ensures that packets are sent at a consistent rate, avoiding overrun conditions that would otherwise cause dropped packets. In shaping configurations, excess packets are queued and transmitted later rather than being discarded, preserving packet integrity and improving the reliability of transmission.

Another important QoS method in WANs is queuing, especially Class-Based Weighted Fair Queuing or Low Latency Queuing. These queuing mechanisms allow the router to prioritize traffic based on its classification. Delay-sensitive traffic such as VoIP is placed in a high-priority queue, ensuring it is forwarded ahead of less critical data. Meanwhile, transactional traffic such as database queries may be assigned a medium priority, while best-effort traffic like email or web browsing is handled in a lower-priority queue. The ability to allocate bandwidth and control delay for different traffic classes ensures that the most important applications receive the network performance they require even during periods of congestion.

Policing is sometimes used in WANs to enforce contractual bandwidth limits, particularly in service provider environments. While shaping is typically preferred because it buffers excess traffic, policing is more rigid and drops or re-marks packets that exceed defined thresholds. In customer environments, policing may be used to prevent certain types of traffic from exceeding a set limit or to ensure fair use among multiple branches sharing a central connection. However, due to the risk of packet loss and its potential impact on real-time applications, policing must be applied carefully and typically to less sensitive traffic classes.

QoS in WANs also includes strategies for redundancy and reliability. Technologies like Multiprotocol Label Switching (MPLS) often support traffic engineering and fast reroute capabilities, enabling packets to take alternate paths in the event of congestion or failure. When used in conjunction with QoS policies, MPLS can ensure that high-priority traffic continues to flow even when parts of the network are impaired. Similarly, WAN optimization techniques such as compression, caching, and protocol acceleration can reduce the volume of traffic and improve perceived performance, but these methods do not replace QoS. Instead, they complement it by reducing demand on limited WAN resources.

In hybrid WAN environments, where traffic may be sent over both private MPLS circuits and public internet links, QoS becomes even more critical. Software-defined WAN solutions introduce dynamic path selection based on real-time measurements of delay, jitter, and packet loss. These solutions rely on consistent QoS markings to determine which path is most appropriate for each type of traffic. For example, a voice call might be routed over an MPLS link with guaranteed latency, while file backup traffic could be sent over a broadband internet connection. The ability to direct traffic intelligently based on QoS requirements is a key benefit of SD-WAN technologies, but it also requires accurate classification and enforcement of QoS policies across all transport options.

Management and monitoring are vital components of QoS in WAN environments. Visibility into traffic flows, queue utilization, latency statistics, and packet loss trends allows network administrators to verify that QoS policies are working as intended. Tools such as NetFlow, SNMP, IP SLA, and telemetry platforms provide actionable data that can inform adjustments to QoS configurations. If certain applications are experiencing delay or degradation, administrators can review class-of-service mappings, increase bandwidth allocations, or adjust shaping and queuing settings to restore performance.

Effective QoS in WAN environments requires not only technical configuration but also strategic planning. Organizations must define traffic classes based on business needs, determine how much bandwidth each class requires, and ensure that policies are implemented consistently across all network segments. Communication with service providers is essential to confirm that QoS markings are honored and that the agreed-upon class-of-service model is enforced end to end. Without this alignment, QoS policies applied internally may have limited impact once traffic leaves the enterprise network.

As business reliance on WAN connectivity continues to grow, particularly with the rise of cloud services and remote work, the importance of QoS in WAN environments cannot be overstated. It ensures that essential applications remain responsive, that resources are used efficiently, and that user experiences remain consistent regardless of location. By carefully designing and implementing QoS strategies tailored to the unique constraints of WAN infrastructure, organizations can achieve a balance between performance, cost, and reliability that supports both current operations and future growth.

Chapter 28: QoS in LANs and Campus Networks

Quality of Service in local area networks and campus environments is essential for delivering reliable and consistent performance across a wide array of applications and services. Unlike wide area networks, LANs generally offer higher bandwidth and lower latency. However, the increasing density of devices, the diversity of traffic types, and the rise of latency-sensitive applications make QoS just as important within the LAN as it is across longer-distance connections. In a campus network, which often encompasses multiple buildings and departments connected through high-speed backbone links, QoS ensures that critical services are prioritized and that users experience consistent application performance regardless of their physical location within the network.

In LAN environments, one of the primary objectives of QoS is to differentiate traffic according to its importance and performance requirements. This begins with accurate classification, which is usually performed at the access layer, where endpoints such as phones, computers, printers, and wireless devices connect to the network. Classification may be based on Layer 2 information such as MAC address or VLAN, Layer 3 data like IP addresses, or Layer 4 characteristics including TCP/UDP ports. Once classified, packets can be marked using Class of Service values in Ethernet frames or DSCP values in IP headers, enabling subsequent devices to apply consistent QoS treatment.

At the core of a campus network, high-speed switches and routers typically support multiple hardware queues, each of which can be configured to process packets differently based on their markings. QoS policies at this level govern how packets are queued, scheduled, and forwarded. For instance, real-time voice and video traffic can be placed in a low-latency queue to ensure prompt delivery, while best-effort data such as email or file downloads is handled with standard forwarding. This separation prevents less critical traffic from interfering with applications that depend on minimal delay and jitter.

One of the key advantages in a LAN or campus environment is the availability of sufficient bandwidth, often measured in gigabits or even tens of gigabits per second. However, even with abundant capacity, congestion can occur at aggregation points, uplinks, and during peak usage times. Without QoS mechanisms, a burst of high-volume traffic such as a large file transfer can temporarily flood an interface, resulting in dropped packets and delayed delivery of more important data. QoS prevents this by enforcing bandwidth reservations and ensuring that each class of traffic receives its fair share of resources. Queuing techniques such as weighted round robin, strict priority queuing, and class-based weighted fair queuing are commonly used to manage this behavior.

Another critical aspect of QoS in LANs is traffic policing and shaping. Although shaping is more common in WANs, it can also be beneficial in campus networks, particularly when coordinating with uplink speeds or preparing traffic for exit to external networks. Policing, on the other hand, may be used within the LAN to enforce rate limits for certain types of traffic. For example, guest wireless traffic might be policed to prevent it from overwhelming internal resources, while internal application servers might be allowed greater access. These enforcement mechanisms help maintain performance and ensure that network usage aligns with organizational policies.

Multicast traffic presents another important use case for QoS in campus networks. Applications such as IPTV, conferencing, and enterprise video streams often rely on multicast to efficiently distribute content to multiple endpoints. Without QoS, multicast traffic can consume excessive bandwidth and affect other services. By applying QoS policies specifically designed for multicast streams, network administrators can prioritize these flows and ensure they do not interfere with unicast applications. Switches and routers in campus networks typically support IGMP snooping and PIM protocols, which, when combined with QoS, enable intelligent and controlled multicast delivery.

Wireless networks are an increasingly integral part of campus environments, and they bring their own set of challenges to QoS. Wireless access points must contend with shared spectrum, variable signal strength, and client mobility. These factors make wireless traffic inherently less predictable and more susceptible to congestion. To address this, modern wireless QoS frameworks such as Wi-Fi Multimedia (WMM) classify traffic into access categories like voice, video, best effort, and background. These categories map to different transmit queues, allowing high-priority packets to contend more aggressively for airtime. Coordinating QoS between the wired and wireless segments of the campus network is essential to maintain consistent service levels.

Another important consideration in campus QoS is the integration of security and access control with traffic management. Many enterprise networks use technologies such as 802.1X authentication, network access control, and segmentation to enforce security policies. These mechanisms can be leveraged in QoS configurations to apply different treatment to different user roles or device types. For instance, authenticated employees may receive higher priority access than guest users, or traffic from trusted IoT devices may be prioritized over unknown endpoints. By integrating QoS with identity and access frameworks, administrators can enforce policies that are both performance-aware and security-conscious.

Visibility and monitoring play a central role in maintaining effective QoS in campus networks. Even with well-designed policies, network conditions change over time, and performance can degrade if adjustments are not made. Tools such as NetFlow, SNMP, and real-time analytics platforms provide detailed insight into traffic patterns, queue utilization, and application behavior. These tools enable administrators to verify that QoS policies are being enforced, detect anomalies, and make informed decisions about resource allocation. Additionally, they support capacity planning by highlighting areas where additional bandwidth or improved policy granularity may be needed.

In multi-vendor environments, interoperability is another consideration. While QoS standards such as DSCP and CoS are widely supported, differences in implementation can lead to inconsistent behavior across platforms. Ensuring that QoS policies are harmonized across all devices and that markings are interpreted consistently is essential for end-to-end service assurance. This includes not only routers and switches but also firewalls, wireless controllers, and endpoint devices, all of which play a role in the QoS ecosystem.

As more applications move to the cloud and more users access services remotely, the campus network becomes the primary conduit for connecting users to mission-critical resources. This shift increases the importance of ensuring that the LAN and campus infrastructure can support high-performance, low-latency communication. QoS helps maintain responsiveness for real-time services, prioritize business-critical applications, and enforce fair usage across diverse user groups and devices. By deploying a thoughtful and comprehensive QoS strategy, organizations can ensure that their campus networks remain robust, efficient, and capable of supporting the demands of a digital-first world.

Chapter 29: QoS in Wireless Networks

Quality of Service in wireless networks has become a fundamental requirement as more critical applications rely on wireless connectivity for real-time communication, cloud access, collaboration, and mobility. Unlike wired networks, which benefit from dedicated bandwidth and more predictable transmission characteristics, wireless networks operate in a shared medium subject to interference, signal degradation, variable client behavior, and fluctuating load conditions. These factors introduce unique challenges that must be addressed through specific QoS mechanisms designed to prioritize traffic, manage contention, and ensure acceptable performance for latency-sensitive services like voice, video, and real-time collaboration.

Wireless QoS begins with the realization that not all traffic is equal and that treating all packets the same in a congested or shared medium inevitably leads to poor user experience. Applications such as Voice over IP and video conferencing require low latency and jitter, while services like email or file downloads can tolerate higher delay. QoS mechanisms in wireless networks aim to distinguish between these types of traffic and prioritize those with more stringent performance requirements. This differentiation is typically achieved through classification, marking, queuing, and scheduling processes that must be adapted to the unique characteristics of wireless transmission.

The IEEE 802.11e standard introduced critical enhancements to enable QoS over Wi-Fi by defining the Wi-Fi Multimedia (WMM) framework. WMM classifies wireless traffic into four access categories: voice, video, best effort, and background. Each category is assigned different transmission parameters such as contention window size, arbitration interframe spacing, and transmission opportunity limits. These parameters control how frequently a device can contend for access to the wireless medium and how much data it can send when it gains access. Voice traffic receives the most aggressive parameters, allowing it to transmit more quickly and more frequently than other types of traffic, thereby reducing delay and jitter.

In practice, QoS in wireless networks begins at the point of traffic classification, typically at the client device or the access point. Traffic is identified based on source and destination IP addresses, protocol type, port numbers, or application signatures. Once classified, packets are mapped to the appropriate WMM category. For example, a VoIP packet might be assigned to the voice access category, while a video stream might go to the video category. Packets that do not match specific criteria are usually assigned to the best effort category, and low-priority traffic such as system updates or large background transfers is sent using the background category. This mapping ensures that time-sensitive traffic receives expedited access to the wireless medium.

One challenge in wireless QoS is the lack of centralized coordination for medium access. Unlike wired switches that can prioritize traffic through dedicated output queues, wireless access points must rely on contention-based mechanisms to share the medium among multiple clients. This means that even if a packet is marked for high priority, it must still compete with other packets for transmission opportunities. The WMM framework addresses this by adjusting the backoff timers and retry behavior for each access category, effectively giving higher priority traffic a better chance of winning contention. However, this is not absolute and does not guarantee bandwidth or delay, especially in high-density environments.

Client behavior also affects QoS implementation. Not all devices support WMM, and among those that do, not all implement it correctly. A client that fails to mark its packets properly or that uses the highest priority for all traffic can disrupt the fairness and effectiveness of the QoS system. This is why it is important for access points to enforce QoS policies, including re-marking traffic based on known application types or enforcing airtime fairness policies. Some advanced wireless systems use deep packet inspection and policy-based classification at the access point level to override incorrect client behavior and ensure that QoS is applied consistently across the network.

Airtime fairness is another critical concept in wireless QoS. Since all clients share the same frequency band, a single slow or poorly performing client can consume a disproportionate amount of airtime, reducing the throughput available for faster clients. This is particularly problematic in mixed environments where legacy devices operate alongside newer, faster clients. QoS mechanisms must account for this by allocating airtime based on client capabilities, signal strength, and traffic priority. Some systems implement airtime-based scheduling, where the access point controls how long each client can transmit, ensuring that high-priority traffic from high-performing clients is not delayed by less efficient transmissions.

Roaming also complicates QoS in wireless environments. As users move through a campus or office space, their devices may roam from one access point to another. Maintaining consistent QoS treatment during these transitions requires that QoS policies be enforced uniformly across the entire wireless infrastructure. This includes maintaining traffic classification, priority mappings, and queue states during the handoff process. Modern wireless architectures often include centralized controllers that manage policy enforcement and ensure that QoS settings persist as users move across the network.

Integration between wireless QoS and the wired network is essential for end-to-end service quality. Once a wireless packet reaches the access point, it is forwarded into the wired network, where it must retain its QoS marking and continue to receive appropriate treatment. This requires consistent configuration of QoS policies across access points, switches, routers, and firewalls. For example, DSCP values marked on wireless traffic should be respected and acted upon by downstream devices to preserve prioritization. Discrepancies between wireless and wired QoS settings can undermine the effectiveness of the entire system.

Wireless QoS also plays a significant role in supporting real-time and mission-critical applications in modern enterprises. Unified communications platforms, including voice, video, chat, and presence services, are heavily dependent on consistent network performance. In healthcare, manufacturing, and education, where mobility and reliability are critical, QoS ensures that vital applications are not disrupted by background traffic or unregulated client behavior. With the increasing adoption of wireless point-of-sale systems, smart sensors, and mobile workforces, the importance of stable and predictable wireless performance continues to grow.

To ensure the effectiveness of QoS in wireless networks, continuous monitoring and management are necessary. Wireless management platforms offer insights into access point utilization, client behavior, queue statistics, and application performance. These tools allow administrators to detect issues such as excessive retries, packet drops, or misbehaving clients and to take corrective actions. Additionally, policy adjustments can be made dynamically based on usage patterns, allowing for adaptive QoS strategies that respond to the changing needs of users and applications.

As wireless technology continues to evolve with standards like Wi-Fi 6 and Wi-Fi 7, QoS mechanisms are becoming more intelligent and efficient. These newer standards introduce features such as orthogonal frequency division multiple access and target wake time, which enhance the ability to manage traffic and reduce contention. QoS will remain a critical component in leveraging these advancements, ensuring that the wireless medium can support the demands of high-density, high-performance, and real-time applications with the same level of reliability and control traditionally found in wired networks.

Chapter 30: MPLS and QoS Integration

Multiprotocol Label Switching, or MPLS, is a high-performance data-carrying technique that plays a significant role in modern enterprise and service provider networks. It was originally developed to speed up network traffic flow and improve routing efficiency, but it has since evolved into a powerful tool for implementing Quality of Service policies across large-scale, multi-service networks. The integration of MPLS and QoS provides a robust framework for delivering differentiated service levels, supporting critical applications, and ensuring that network resources are used effectively and fairly. By combining the traffic engineering capabilities of MPLS with the control and prioritization mechanisms of QoS, organizations can meet stringent service-level agreements and maintain consistent performance even under challenging network conditions.

At the core of MPLS is the concept of label switching. Instead of forwarding packets based solely on destination IP addresses, MPLS assigns a short, fixed-length label to each packet as it enters the network. These labels are used by MPLS-enabled routers, known as

Label Switch Routers, to make forwarding decisions without consulting complex routing tables. The label essentially serves as an index into a forwarding table, streamlining packet processing and reducing latency. This labeling system allows MPLS to support multiple traffic paths and classes, making it an ideal environment for integrating QoS mechanisms.

In MPLS networks, QoS is implemented primarily through the use of the Traffic Class field, which occupies three bits in the MPLS header. This field, formerly known as the EXP or experimental field, supports up to eight traffic classes, allowing packets to be classified and prioritized as they traverse the MPLS domain. The Traffic Class field can be derived from IP-level markings such as DSCP or IP Precedence, providing a seamless transition from traditional IP QoS models into the MPLS infrastructure. Once packets are marked, MPLS routers can apply different queuing, scheduling, and drop policies based on the value of the Traffic Class field.

One of the most important benefits of MPLS and QoS integration is the ability to perform traffic engineering. Traffic engineering enables network operators to control the path that traffic takes through the network based on resource availability, policy constraints, and application requirements. This is particularly useful in congested or complex networks, where shortest-path routing may not always yield the best performance. With MPLS, operators can establish Label Switched Paths that are optimized for specific traffic types, ensuring that high-priority applications receive low-latency, low-loss treatment even when alternative paths are more efficient for other types of traffic.

MPLS QoS is often used to support differentiated services models within service provider environments. Customers may subscribe to multiple classes of service, each with its own performance guarantees. For example, a business might purchase premium bandwidth for VoIP and video conferencing traffic, standard service for transactional applications, and best-effort service for non-critical data. Within the MPLS domain, these service levels are mapped to specific Traffic Class values, allowing routers to prioritize, queue, and forward packets accordingly. This allows providers to offer tiered services and enforce service-level agreements with precision and scalability.

The use of MPLS also enhances the predictability and manageability of QoS. Because Label Switched Paths are explicitly defined and controlled, network operators have greater visibility into traffic flows and can allocate resources more effectively. Congestion can be minimized by distributing traffic evenly across available paths, and critical applications can be routed over links with the most available bandwidth and lowest latency. Additionally, MPLS provides mechanisms for preemptive rerouting in the event of link failure or degradation, ensuring that QoS commitments are maintained even during network disruptions.

Integrating QoS with MPLS also requires careful coordination between edge and core devices. Traffic classification and marking typically occur at the network edge, where packets are inspected and assigned a Traffic Class based on application type, source, destination, or other criteria. These markings are then used by core routers to make forwarding and scheduling decisions without re-examining the packet's payload. This division of labor reduces processing overhead in the core and improves overall network scalability. However, it also means that accurate and consistent classification at the edge is essential for QoS policies to be effective.

In practice, MPLS networks often implement queuing strategies such as Class-Based Weighted Fair Queuing or Strict Priority Queuing based on Traffic Class values. These queues determine the order in which packets are forwarded and how bandwidth is allocated among different classes. For example, voice traffic may be placed in a high-priority queue with strict scheduling to ensure minimal delay, while data traffic is managed in lower-priority queues with fair-share algorithms. Drop policies such as Weighted Random Early Detection may also be applied to prevent congestion by proactively discarding lower-priority packets when queue thresholds are exceeded.

Another aspect of MPLS QoS integration is the use of policing and shaping mechanisms. Policing ensures that traffic entering the network conforms to the agreed-upon rate for its class of service. If the traffic exceeds this rate, excess packets may be dropped or re-marked to a lower class. Shaping, on the other hand, smooths traffic bursts by delaying packets to maintain a consistent transmission rate. These controls help preserve QoS guarantees within the MPLS network and ensure fair resource usage across multiple customers and services.

For organizations deploying MPLS-based QoS, monitoring and visibility are critical components of success. Network operators must be able to track performance metrics such as latency, jitter, packet loss, and utilization by class of service. Tools such as NetFlow, SNMP, and performance monitoring protocols provide the data needed to validate QoS policies, identify issues, and make informed adjustments. Real-time telemetry can enhance this visibility by offering granular, actionable insights into traffic behavior, enabling faster response to changing conditions and more effective network optimization.

As enterprises increasingly adopt hybrid and cloud-based architectures, MPLS continues to play a key role in delivering reliable and secure connectivity. MPLS QoS ensures that mission-critical traffic receives the necessary treatment, even across long distances and heterogeneous environments. While newer technologies such as SD-WAN offer additional flexibility and cost advantages, many of these platforms still rely on MPLS as part of their transport strategy, making the integration of MPLS and QoS a foundational skill for network engineers and architects.

MPLS and QoS integration creates a powerful synergy that enhances the performance, reliability, and predictability of IP networks. By leveraging MPLS's traffic engineering capabilities and combining them with advanced QoS controls, organizations can deliver consistent service quality across complex topologies and diverse application requirements. This integration supports not only operational efficiency and user satisfaction but also the ability to offer differentiated services and maintain competitive advantage in a data-driven world.

Chapter 31: QoS in VoIP and Real-Time Applications

Quality of Service in Voice over IP and other real-time applications is essential to ensure the delivery of high-quality, uninterrupted communication experiences across IP networks. Unlike traditional data traffic, which can tolerate some delays, jitter, or retransmissions, real-time applications are sensitive to even small variations in network behavior. Voice, video conferencing, remote desktop sessions, and collaborative tools all rely on low latency, low jitter, minimal packet loss, and consistent throughput. The unpredictable nature of IP networks, where traffic can vary in volume and destination, makes QoS a critical component for supporting these delay-sensitive services.

VoIP is one of the most demanding applications in terms of QoS. A typical VoIP packet is small, and the intervals between packets are tightly controlled to ensure natural, real-time communication. If packets arrive late or out of order, the audio can sound choppy, distorted, or robotic. If packets are lost entirely and cannot be reconstructed by jitter buffers, the user hears dropouts or missing syllables. Because VoIP traffic is also bi-directional and interactive, poor quality on either leg of the communication can compromise the entire experience. These challenges are magnified when VoIP is deployed over shared networks where bandwidth must be managed across multiple applications and users.

To address these challenges, QoS for VoIP starts with proper classification. Traffic must be identified as voice traffic as early as possible, typically at the point where it enters the network. This can be achieved by inspecting port numbers used by signaling protocols like SIP or RTP or by identifying endpoints such as IP phones. Once classified, the traffic is marked using Layer 2 or Layer 3 identifiers such as Class of Service values or DSCP tags. The recommended DSCP value for VoIP is 46, which corresponds to Expedited Forwarding. This marking ensures that intermediate network devices recognize the traffic as high priority and treat it accordingly throughout its journey.

After classification and marking, VoIP traffic must be placed into appropriate queues to ensure it is forwarded with minimal delay. This is commonly achieved using Low Latency Queuing, where VoIP packets are placed in a strict priority queue that is serviced before all other traffic classes. The priority queue is often policed to prevent it from being overwhelmed by misclassified traffic or by excessive voice traffic volumes. This policing guarantees that other classes of service are not starved of bandwidth while ensuring that real-time traffic receives the low delay it requires. Proper configuration of these queues is critical, as misplacement or improper prioritization can degrade voice quality.

In addition to queuing, shaping and traffic engineering also contribute to QoS for real-time applications. Shaping is used to smooth traffic bursts and ensure that the sending rate matches the capacity of downstream links. This prevents packet drops at congestion points and reduces jitter. In WAN environments, where bandwidth is often limited, shaping VoIP traffic to a consistent rate can help ensure it receives uninterrupted service. Traffic engineering techniques, such as MPLS Label Switched Paths or SD-WAN dynamic path selection, can steer real-time traffic onto paths with the lowest latency and loss, further improving performance.

Jitter buffers also play a role in supporting VoIP quality. These buffers temporarily store arriving packets and reorder them to compensate for variations in arrival time. While jitter buffers help smooth playback, they introduce additional delay, so their size must be carefully balanced. Too small a buffer may not compensate for jitter, while too large a buffer increases latency and affects the responsiveness of the conversation. Network QoS mechanisms aim to minimize jitter upstream so that jitter buffers can operate effectively without excessive delay.

Packet loss is another critical issue for VoIP. Unlike file transfers or web traffic, voice packets are not retransmitted if lost, as retransmissions would arrive too late to be useful. Therefore, it is essential to design networks and apply QoS policies that prevent congestion and reduce the likelihood of packet drops. Techniques such as Weighted Random Early Detection can be used in lower-priority queues to discard traffic early and avoid congestion in queues serving high-priority real-time traffic. Network monitoring tools can be used to track loss rates, identify problem areas, and inform adjustments to QoS policies.

Video conferencing presents many of the same challenges as VoIP, but with added complexity. Video traffic typically consumes more bandwidth and is more variable in nature. Unlike voice, which has a relatively constant bit rate, video traffic can spike during periods of increased motion or screen changes. QoS policies for video must therefore accommodate this variability by allowing higher peak rates or by shaping traffic based on expected behavior. Video streams are typically marked with DSCP values such as 34, corresponding to Assured Forwarding classes with higher drop precedence than voice but still prioritized above best-effort traffic. These values allow the network to differentiate between audio and video within the same session and allocate resources accordingly.

Collaboration platforms, which combine voice, video, screen sharing, and messaging, require coordinated QoS treatment across multiple traffic types. Each media stream must be identified and prioritized based on its sensitivity to delay and loss. For example, screen sharing may be marked and queued as a lower-priority flow compared to voice and video, but higher than background file transfers. This multi-stream awareness requires sophisticated classification and queuing policies, especially in environments where bandwidth must be shared across many concurrent sessions.

Mobility introduces further complexity to QoS for real-time applications. As users move between access points or network segments, their sessions must maintain QoS treatment. Wireless networks use standards like WMM to apply prioritization at the air interface, while backend network infrastructure must preserve QoS markings and reapply policy at each new connection point. Seamless handoff and session continuity are essential to maintain audio and video quality without interruptions or degradation.

Security appliances such as firewalls and VPN concentrators must also be QoS-aware. They must maintain DSCP markings through encrypted tunnels or reapply them at the tunnel endpoint. If markings are stripped or not honored, the QoS policy breaks down and real-time application performance suffers. Therefore, end-to-end QoS design must include all network elements, from endpoint to access layer, core, edge, and across WAN or cloud links. Consistent configuration and policy enforcement across devices and domains are necessary to deliver the expected performance.

Network administrators must monitor real-time traffic performance continuously. Metrics such as Mean Opinion Score, jitter, latency, packet loss, and call completion rates provide insights into the effectiveness of QoS policies. These metrics can be collected using protocols such as IP SLA or through unified communication monitoring tools. Based on this data, QoS configurations can be fine-tuned to address emerging issues or accommodate changing usage patterns.

Supporting VoIP and real-time applications over IP networks is a complex but necessary task in modern organizations. With the right QoS strategies, traffic can be prioritized, bandwidth can be used efficiently, and user experience can remain consistent even under varying network loads. Voice, video, and collaborative applications have become essential to daily operations, and ensuring their performance through QoS is no longer optional—it is a requirement for operational success.

Chapter 32: QoS for Video Streaming

Quality of Service for video streaming plays a vital role in delivering smooth, high-quality video experiences across IP networks. Unlike traditional file downloads or email traffic, which are resilient to delay and packet loss due to retransmission mechanisms, video streaming applications require timely and consistent delivery of data to maintain uninterrupted playback. Video traffic presents unique challenges because it is typically high-bandwidth, time-sensitive, and subject to fluctuations in bit rate depending on compression algorithms, screen content, and user interactions. As streaming video becomes a dominant source of network traffic across enterprise, educational, and entertainment sectors, implementing effective QoS strategies has become increasingly critical for network administrators and service providers.

Video streaming can be broadly categorized into two models: live streaming and on-demand streaming. Live streaming, such as webinars, virtual meetings, and broadcast events, requires near real-time delivery with minimal buffering and delay. On-demand streaming, which includes services like Netflix, YouTube, or corporate training videos, typically relies on buffering and adaptive bit rate techniques to mitigate variability in network conditions. While both models benefit from QoS, live video places a stronger emphasis on low latency and jitter control, whereas on-demand video places more weight on consistent throughput and minimal packet loss. QoS policies must account for these differences and be designed to support the expected behavior of each type of stream.

The first step in implementing QoS for video streaming is traffic classification. This involves identifying video traffic as it enters the network and separating it from other types of traffic such as voice, web browsing, or file transfers. Classification can be done based on source and destination IP addresses, TCP/UDP port numbers, or application-layer inspection. For example, streaming traffic from known media servers or cloud video services can be matched using access control lists or deep packet inspection. Once classified, the video packets are marked with appropriate DSCP values, typically in the Assured Forwarding class, such as AF41 or AF42, depending on their priority and sensitivity to loss. These markings enable downstream network devices to recognize and apply correct treatment to the video flows.

After marking, video traffic must be managed through proper queuing mechanisms. In environments where bandwidth is constrained or contention is likely, video traffic should be placed in a dedicated queue that guarantees a minimum amount of bandwidth and prevents it from being delayed by less sensitive traffic. Class-Based Weighted Fair Queuing is a commonly used mechanism that allows video to coexist with voice and data while ensuring that it receives a proportional share of resources. Unlike voice, which is usually assigned to a strict priority queue, video is better served in a high-bandwidth, low-drop precedence queue that allows it to burst during periods of increased activity while still maintaining fairness.

Queuing alone is not sufficient to guarantee video quality, especially in networks where congestion is a frequent issue. Shaping and policing mechanisms must also be considered. Shaping is particularly useful on egress interfaces where high-volume video streams are sent over links with limited capacity. It buffers excess packets and transmits them at a steady rate, smoothing out bursts and preventing downstream devices from becoming overwhelmed. This is especially relevant when sending video across WAN or internet links, where bandwidth must be carefully managed. Policing, by contrast, is used to enforce rate limits by discarding or remarking packets that exceed the allowed threshold. For video, excessive policing can degrade quality significantly, so it must be applied cautiously and typically only to non-critical or background video content.

Adaptive Bitrate Streaming is a technique commonly used by modern video platforms to adjust the quality of the video in real time based on available bandwidth and device performance. This technique helps mitigate the effects of congestion by lowering the bit rate when necessary, thus reducing the load on the network. However, adaptive streaming still requires consistent delivery of data chunks to avoid buffering and playback interruptions. QoS mechanisms must ensure that even lower-resolution streams are delivered reliably, especially in environments with many concurrent users. Network policies can be configured to detect adaptive streaming flows and prioritize them according to their current bitrate and user category.

Wireless networks introduce additional complexity for video streaming QoS. Video is one of the most demanding applications in Wi-Fi environments due to its high data rate and susceptibility to interference and contention. Wireless QoS standards like Wi-Fi Multimedia allow video traffic to be classified into the video access category, which gives it preferential access to the medium over best-effort or background traffic. Access points must be configured to recognize DSCP or IP-based policies and map them appropriately to WMM queues. Additionally, airtime fairness and bandwidth steering techniques can be used to ensure that high-bandwidth video clients do not starve other users or suffer due to slow clients occupying excessive airtime.

Monitoring is essential to ensure that QoS for video streaming is working as intended. Metrics such as throughput, jitter, packet loss, and buffer status should be continuously tracked. Real-time analytics tools can detect when video streams are experiencing degradation and alert administrators to potential issues. Packet capture and flow analysis can be used to identify specific streams that are being dropped, delayed, or improperly marked. Visibility into application behavior helps administrators tune QoS policies to changing usage patterns and traffic loads, ensuring that the most critical video applications continue to perform optimally.

Integration with other QoS domains is also important. In a corporate environment, video may traverse multiple segments, including wireless LANs, wired LANs, WAN links, VPN tunnels, and cloud provider backbones. Consistency in marking, queuing, and bandwidth allocation across all these domains is critical for end-to-end performance. DSCP values set at the video source must be preserved or remapped accurately by all intermediary devices. If any segment strips markings or fails to prioritize video correctly, the entire QoS strategy may be compromised.

Video streaming QoS also has a strategic impact on digital transformation initiatives. As more training, communication, and collaboration shift to video-centric platforms, ensuring that these services operate smoothly is essential to productivity and user satisfaction. In education, students rely on uninterrupted video to engage in virtual learning. In healthcare, telemedicine sessions must be clear and real-time. In enterprise, executive broadcasts, onboarding videos, and collaborative meetings depend on network conditions that support high-definition video without interruptions. QoS is not simply a technical enhancement in these scenarios—it becomes a business enabler.

As video continues to grow in volume and importance, network infrastructures must be designed to support its specific needs. QoS policies must evolve with traffic patterns, codec advancements, and user expectations. With proper classification, marking, queuing, shaping, and monitoring, networks can deliver reliable and high-quality video streaming services, even under challenging conditions. Investing in QoS for video streaming is no longer optional for organizations seeking to remain competitive and connected in a digital-first world.

Chapter 33: QoS for Cloud Services and SaaS

Quality of Service for cloud services and Software as a Service platforms has become an essential requirement for organizations relying on digital transformation and cloud-first strategies. As businesses shift from on-premises applications to hosted services accessed over the internet or private connections, the performance of these services becomes highly dependent on the quality and predictability of the network. SaaS applications such as Microsoft 365, Google Workspace, Salesforce, and other business-critical platforms require consistent and reliable connectivity to deliver a seamless user experience. Even minor fluctuations in latency, jitter, or packet loss can disrupt user workflows, reduce productivity, and undermine confidence in the platform. QoS mechanisms are necessary to prioritize cloud-bound traffic, allocate bandwidth appropriately, and ensure that cloud services receive the performance they require alongside other enterprise applications.

One of the primary challenges in delivering QoS for cloud services is the lack of direct administrative control over the application hosting environment. Unlike traditional applications where the organization controls both the server and client environments, SaaS operates in a multi-tenant cloud infrastructure where the service provider manages the backend. This shifts the focus of QoS implementation to the enterprise's internal network and its connection to the cloud. Traffic shaping, queuing, and prioritization must be applied to outbound and inbound flows that travel through firewalls, WAN links, and internet gateways. These network segments become the chokepoints that determine whether cloud application traffic arrives in a timely and reliable manner.

Traffic classification is the first step in establishing QoS for cloud services. It involves identifying SaaS traffic at the point of entry into the network, typically at the branch router or data center edge. Because SaaS traffic may be encrypted and share ports with other web traffic, traditional methods of classification based on TCP/UDP ports are often insufficient. Instead, organizations increasingly rely on DNS-based identification, IP reputation databases, or application-aware firewalls to detect and classify traffic destined for specific SaaS providers. Once identified, traffic can be tagged with DSCP values to reflect its priority. For instance, collaboration platforms that include voice and video components may be marked with Expedited Forwarding, while interactive web applications might be marked with Assured Forwarding, and non-essential cloud traffic could remain best effort.

After classification and marking, traffic is subject to queuing and scheduling policies that control how packets are forwarded across congested links. Class-Based Weighted Fair Queuing is commonly used to manage SaaS traffic alongside voice, video, and bulk data. The goal is to ensure that cloud application flows are not delayed behind large file transfers or background traffic. By allocating a minimum amount of bandwidth to SaaS traffic and allowing it to burst when needed, queuing policies help preserve user experience during times of network contention. In some implementations, SaaS traffic is given a dedicated queue or treated as a separate traffic class, allowing for more granular monitoring and control.

Shaping is also an important tool in managing SaaS traffic. Particularly in WAN environments or SD-WAN architectures, shaping ensures that the transmission rate of cloud-bound traffic aligns with the available bandwidth on internet or MPLS links. Shaping prevents packet drops caused by sudden traffic bursts and allows for smooth transitions between different service types. For example, during peak hours, an organization may shape software update traffic or file synchronization processes to prevent them from interfering with interactive SaaS usage. This time-sensitive shaping allows administrators to prioritize real-time interactions while still permitting background cloud tasks to proceed at a controlled rate.

SD-WAN has emerged as a transformative technology in the context of QoS for cloud services. By abstracting the underlying transport and allowing for dynamic path selection, SD-WAN enables organizations to steer cloud traffic across the most appropriate links based on real-time performance metrics. Policies can be defined to send mission-critical SaaS applications over MPLS links with guaranteed performance or over broadband internet connections when appropriate. SD-WAN solutions continuously monitor path conditions such as latency, jitter, and loss, dynamically rerouting traffic when thresholds are exceeded. This capability enhances the QoS experience for cloud users without requiring constant manual intervention.

Another critical consideration in SaaS QoS is peering and direct connectivity with cloud providers. Many cloud vendors offer dedicated connectivity options such as Azure ExpressRoute, AWS Direct Connect, or Google Cloud Interconnect. These services bypass the public internet and provide more predictable performance through private, managed circuits. By integrating these services into the enterprise network and applying QoS policies to the ingress and egress points, organizations can extend their QoS strategy into the cloud provider's network. This tightens control over performance and reduces the variability associated with public internet transport.

Visibility and monitoring are essential for maintaining QoS in cloud-centric environments. Network administrators must be able to distinguish between different types of cloud traffic, assess performance, and identify bottlenecks. Tools such as deep packet inspection, NetFlow analysis, and cloud access security brokers provide detailed insight into application usage and behavior. Performance monitoring platforms can measure round-trip time, DNS resolution latency, and throughput for specific SaaS applications, enabling proactive detection of issues before they affect users. With this data, policies can be fine-tuned to adapt to changing usage patterns, seasonal traffic spikes, or new cloud services introduced into the environment.

Security considerations also intersect with QoS for cloud services. Many enterprises use cloud proxies, VPNs, and firewalls to inspect and secure outbound traffic. These devices must be QoS-aware to preserve performance for cloud applications. If traffic is re-encrypted or tunneled, QoS markings must be maintained or re-applied at tunnel endpoints. Misconfigured security devices can introduce latency, strip DSCP values, or interfere with traffic classification, negating the benefits of a carefully designed QoS policy. Ensuring that security and QoS policies work together is critical for achieving both performance and protection.

End-user experience is the ultimate measure of success for QoS in SaaS environments. Even with high bandwidth availability, inconsistent application responsiveness, login delays, or page timeouts can frustrate users and reduce productivity. QoS policies must account for not only the data flows but also the behaviors and expectations of users. By prioritizing traffic based on business impact and user role, organizations can ensure that executives, developers, customer service agents, and other critical staff receive the performance needed to carry out their responsibilities effectively.

In the cloud era, network performance becomes the backbone of digital experience. With more applications migrating to SaaS models and more workflows depending on cloud connectivity, QoS is no longer optional. It is a necessity for ensuring continuity, competitiveness, and customer satisfaction. From the first DNS query to the last byte of a session, every aspect of cloud traffic must be understood, classified, and treated with the appropriate level of care. Organizations that invest in robust QoS strategies for cloud and SaaS applications are better positioned to meet user expectations, reduce support overhead, and fully capitalize on the promise of cloud computing.

Chapter 34: QoS in Mobile and 5G Networks

Quality of Service in mobile and 5G networks represents a critical layer of intelligence that enables the delivery of diverse services with highly variable requirements on a shared and dynamic radio access infrastructure. Unlike traditional fixed-line networks, mobile environments are characterized by constant movement, fluctuating signal conditions, limited radio spectrum, and rapidly changing traffic loads. These characteristics make QoS not just a performance optimization tool, but an essential component of network architecture. With the introduction of 5G, which brings promises of ultra-low latency, high bandwidth, and massive device connectivity, the importance of QoS has expanded dramatically. It now supports not only human-centric applications like video calls and streaming but also machine-type communications, industrial automation, augmented reality, and autonomous vehicles.

QoS in mobile networks has traditionally relied on standardized classes of service, which define specific treatment for different types of traffic. These classes are implemented through a combination of scheduling, prioritization, and resource allocation mechanisms at various layers of the network. In 4G LTE, for example, the Evolved

Packet System uses bearers to carry traffic flows, with each bearer assigned a QoS Class Identifier that determines its handling across the network. These identifiers control parameters such as maximum bit rate, guaranteed bit rate, packet delay budget, and packet error loss rate. By mapping application traffic to the appropriate bearer, the network ensures that voice calls, web browsing, video playback, and background synchronization all receive treatment aligned with their technical requirements.

With 5G, QoS becomes even more granular and dynamic. The 5G system introduces a Service-Based Architecture that separates control and user plane functions, enabling more flexible and programmable QoS enforcement. At the core of 5G QoS is the concept of QoS Flows, which replace bearers and are identified by a 5G QoS Identifier. These flows are created, modified, and deleted in real time as users move, change applications, or traverse different radio cells. Each QoS Flow can have its own set of parameters, allowing operators to define specific treatment for individual services within the same device or session. This is critical in supporting applications with dramatically different needs, such as a user participating in a video call while simultaneously using navigation, receiving push notifications, and streaming music.

One of the most innovative aspects of 5G QoS is network slicing. A network slice is a virtual network instance that provides an end-to-end logical connection with guaranteed resources and QoS. Each slice can be tailored to a specific use case, such as enhanced mobile broadband, ultra-reliable low latency communication, or massive machine-type communication. For example, a slice for connected vehicles can be configured with extremely low latency and high reliability, while a slice for industrial IoT can prioritize device density and low power consumption. QoS in this context is not just about prioritizing traffic but about allocating dedicated resources, spectrum, and policies across the radio, transport, and core domains to meet strict service-level agreements.

To enforce QoS in mobile and 5G networks, multiple layers of the network participate in decision-making. At the radio access level, base stations or gNodeBs implement scheduling algorithms that decide which user equipment gets access to the air interface at any given time. These algorithms consider factors such as QoS priority level, channel quality, device mobility, and current load conditions. In situations where radio resources are scarce, packets from higher-priority flows are transmitted first, while lower-priority traffic may be delayed or dropped. This real-time decision-making ensures that critical applications such as voice and emergency services maintain integrity even during periods of congestion or interference.

In the transport network, QoS is implemented using standard IP mechanisms such as DSCP marking and traffic engineering. Traffic from different QoS flows is mapped to different queues and paths based on its marking, allowing for differentiated handling as it traverses routers and switches. In 5G, the use of Segment Routing and Software-Defined Networking enhances this capability by enabling more granular path control and dynamic reallocation of resources based on current network state. The control plane can monitor performance metrics such as latency and jitter and adjust flow paths in real time to optimize QoS compliance.

The user plane function in 5G also plays a significant role in QoS enforcement. It performs packet detection, flow classification, and forwarding based on QoS parameters received from the control plane. It ensures that QoS flows are mapped to appropriate bearers and that traffic is shaped or policed to meet configured rates. This layer is responsible for maintaining the consistency of QoS treatment even as users move across different cells or access technologies. Seamless handovers are essential in preserving QoS, especially for latency-sensitive applications like gaming, augmented reality, or VoIP, where even brief interruptions can severely impact the user experience.

Mobility management adds another layer of complexity to QoS in mobile networks. As users move across coverage areas, their traffic must be handed off between base stations, and in some cases, between network slices or even different access technologies. The QoS framework must ensure that the user's traffic maintains the same level of priority and performance during and after the handover. This requires coordination between radio access nodes, core network functions, and policy control mechanisms. Fast handovers and pre-established QoS flows help maintain service continuity and avoid service degradation during movement.

Policy control and charging functions are central to dynamic QoS in mobile and 5G networks. These functions define which subscribers, devices, or applications are entitled to specific QoS levels, based on their subscription plan, usage history, or network conditions. Policies can be triggered by usage thresholds, time of day, location, or congestion status. For instance, premium users may receive guaranteed throughput during busy hours, while standard users are managed on a best-effort basis. In enterprise contexts, different departments or applications can receive differentiated treatment, ensuring that business-critical services remain unaffected by recreational or background traffic.

Security and QoS also intersect in mobile networks. Encrypted traffic, VPNs, and tunneling protocols must be handled in a way that preserves QoS markings and allows for proper classification. Mislabeling or stripping of QoS information can lead to suboptimal treatment and degraded performance. Moreover, networks must protect against abuse, such as unauthorized applications attempting to mark themselves as high priority. Authentication, integrity checks, and policy enforcement mechanisms are needed to ensure that QoS is applied fairly and according to defined rules.

QoS in mobile and 5G networks is no longer limited to voice or video prioritization. It has become an integral part of the overall network architecture, enabling the coexistence of radically different service types on a single infrastructure. From immersive consumer experiences to mission-critical industrial control, every use case demands a specific set of performance guarantees that only a robust and flexible QoS framework can provide. The evolution of mobile networks into fully programmable, service-aware platforms is unlocking new possibilities for innovation, but it also requires careful design, coordination, and ongoing optimization of QoS mechanisms across every layer of the network. In this context, QoS is not just about traffic management but about delivering on the full promise of mobility, connectivity, and digital transformation.

Chapter 35: Policy-Based QoS Management

Policy-based Quality of Service management introduces a structured and scalable approach to enforcing network traffic rules across complex, multi-service environments. As networks continue to expand in size, complexity, and user diversity, manually configuring QoS parameters on each device becomes increasingly impractical and error-prone. Policy-based QoS offers a centralized framework that defines how different types of traffic should be handled under various conditions, enabling network administrators to enforce consistent performance standards, security controls, and resource prioritization across all network segments. It replaces static configurations with dynamic, adaptable rules that reflect business objectives, user roles, application needs, and operational constraints.

At its core, policy-based QoS relies on a policy engine or controller that interprets high-level policies and translates them into device-specific configurations. These policies are written using abstract criteria such as user identity, application type, device group, or time of day rather than low-level technical attributes. This abstraction allows organizations to define traffic-handling behavior in terms of business requirements. For example, a policy might state that executive video calls receive the highest priority at all times, or that guest Wi-Fi traffic is limited to best-effort service during business hours. The system automatically maps these policies to the appropriate queues, markings, and rate limits, removing the need for manual intervention.

The effectiveness of policy-based QoS depends on accurate classification and identification of network traffic. Modern systems use deep packet inspection, behavioral analytics, and metadata analysis to detect and categorize applications in real time. This allows the policy engine to apply the correct rules to each flow as it enters the network. Classification can occur at multiple layers, including access switches, wireless controllers, firewalls, and WAN edge devices. Once classified, traffic is tagged with identifiers such as DSCP values or internal labels that guide its treatment through the network infrastructure. These tags inform queuing, scheduling, shaping, and policing decisions across all downstream devices.

One of the main advantages of policy-based QoS is its adaptability to changing conditions. Because policies are centrally defined and dynamically enforced, they can respond to real-time network metrics such as congestion, link failures, or device availability. For instance, if a WAN link becomes congested, the policy controller can adjust shaping rates or reallocate bandwidth to ensure that high-priority applications remain unaffected. Similarly, policies can be context-aware, adapting to the location of the user, the device in use, or the security posture of the connection. A user accessing corporate resources from a managed laptop on a secure LAN may receive higher QoS treatment than the same user connecting over a mobile network from a personal device.

Policy-based QoS also enhances multi-tenant and multi-domain environments. In shared data centers or service provider networks, different customers or departments may have distinct QoS requirements. Policy frameworks enable the isolation and enforcement of these requirements without manual configuration of each individual flow. By associating policies with virtual network segments, VLANs, or VPN tunnels, administrators can ensure that each tenant receives the service quality they are entitled to, regardless of how the underlying infrastructure is shared. This is particularly useful in cloud, campus, and branch architectures where centralized policy control allows consistent treatment of traffic even as users and applications move across network boundaries.

In addition to controlling traffic flow, policy-based QoS contributes to network security and compliance. Policies can include constraints on application usage, data transfer rates, or geographic access, effectively integrating access control with performance management. For example, a policy may prohibit streaming video on guest networks while allowing business applications to function normally. Another policy may limit data backup operations to overnight hours to preserve bandwidth during the day. These restrictions ensure that network resources are used in alignment with organizational goals while reducing the risk of performance degradation or unauthorized behavior.

Policy enforcement in QoS is typically handled by network devices such as routers, switches, and firewalls that support standardized mechanisms like QoS class maps, policy maps, and service policies. These configurations are often pushed from a central controller using protocols such as NETCONF, REST APIs, or vendor-specific management interfaces. As policies change, the controller updates the device configurations without requiring manual reentry of commands. This level of automation improves agility, reduces configuration errors, and allows organizations to scale QoS management across hundreds or thousands of devices with minimal operational overhead.

Visibility and reporting are integral to policy-based QoS. Administrators need to know not only which policies are in place but also how they are affecting traffic in real time. Dashboards and analytics tools provide insights into policy compliance, application performance, and user experience. Metrics such as latency, jitter, packet loss, and throughput are aggregated and correlated with specific policies to determine their effectiveness. When performance falls below expectations, administrators can drill down into specific flows, users, or devices to identify the root cause and adjust policies accordingly. This feedback loop enables continuous optimization and alignment of QoS policies with organizational priorities.

Policy-based QoS also integrates with broader network automation and orchestration platforms. In software-defined networking environments, QoS policies are often defined as part of the intent-based networking model, where administrators specify desired outcomes rather than specific configurations. The network then interprets this intent and applies the appropriate policies across all infrastructure components. This integration ensures that QoS is not an isolated function but part of a comprehensive approach to network management that includes security, access control, and performance optimization.

As applications continue to evolve and user expectations rise, policy-based QoS provides the flexibility and intelligence needed to support modern networking demands. It allows organizations to align their network behavior with business objectives, ensure fairness and performance across competing services, and maintain control in an increasingly complex and dynamic environment. Whether managing cloud access, voice communication, real-time collaboration, or background data synchronization, policy-based QoS empowers network teams to deliver consistent, high-quality experiences without the burden of manual configuration or constant troubleshooting. It represents a shift from reactive performance management to proactive service assurance, enabling the network to adapt in real time to the needs of users, applications, and the business itself.

Chapter 36: End-to-End QoS Strategies

End-to-end Quality of Service strategies are essential in ensuring that traffic is treated consistently across all segments of a network, from the originating endpoint to the final destination. In today's highly distributed and application-driven environments, network performance is only as good as its weakest link. A seamless QoS experience cannot be achieved by configuring isolated policies on individual devices; instead, it requires a coordinated, holistic approach that integrates access, distribution, core, data center, WAN, wireless, and cloud segments. Each of these domains plays a role in how traffic is classified, prioritized, queued, shaped, and forwarded, and all must work together to meet the performance requirements of critical applications.

The fundamental principle of end-to-end QoS is consistency. From the moment a packet is generated by a client device, it should be identified and marked in a way that reflects its application type and service priority. This initial classification, often performed at the access layer or even at the endpoint itself, sets the tone for how the packet will be treated throughout its journey. Classifying packets based on criteria such as IP addresses, TCP/UDP port numbers, protocol types, or application-level identifiers allows the network to distinguish between voice, video, business-critical data, best-effort traffic, and background processes. Once classified, packets are marked using Layer 2 or Layer 3 QoS fields such as CoS, DSCP, or MPLS EXP, depending on the network architecture.

Maintaining these markings across network boundaries is one of the primary challenges in end-to-end QoS. Each segment of the network, from the campus LAN to the data center and across WAN or internet paths, must honor and interpret these markings consistently. In multi-vendor environments, differences in default QoS behavior can result in mismatched priorities or dropped packets. To avoid this, network administrators must align QoS configurations across all platforms, ensuring that mappings between DSCP and queuing strategies are understood and enforced uniformly. Tools such as QoS trust states, classification policies, and re-marking rules help preserve the integrity of QoS across different segments and technologies.

At the distribution and core layers of the network, the primary focus of QoS shifts from classification to efficient queuing and scheduling. These devices often handle large volumes of traffic and rely on hardware-accelerated queues to maintain performance. High-priority traffic such as voice or control messages is placed into strict-priority queues to guarantee minimal latency and jitter, while video, transactional data, and best-effort flows are assigned to weighted queues that ensure fair bandwidth distribution. Core network devices must be configured to recognize QoS markings and map them to appropriate queues, while also implementing mechanisms such as congestion avoidance and buffer management to prevent degradation during peak usage periods.

In the data center, QoS strategies must accommodate high-speed, low-latency communication between servers, storage, and application services. Virtualization and microservices architectures introduce east-west traffic patterns that require intra-data center QoS in addition to the traditional north-south flows. Technologies such as Data Center Bridging, priority flow control, and application-aware traffic shaping are used to ensure that storage traffic, real-time application flows, and management data coexist without interference. Virtual switches within hypervisors must also be QoS-aware, classifying and marking traffic from virtual machines before it exits the server. In hybrid cloud environments, policies must be extended to virtual networks and cloud-native services to ensure consistency across private and public infrastructure.

The WAN and internet segments introduce unique challenges to end-to-end QoS due to limited bandwidth, higher latency, and variable congestion. Whether using MPLS, SD-WAN, VPN tunnels, or direct internet access, QoS must be enforced on outbound and inbound traffic at the WAN edge. Traffic shaping is often applied to match the egress rate with the available bandwidth, while queuing policies ensure that high-priority traffic is sent first during periods of congestion. With SD-WAN, application-aware routing allows traffic to be dynamically directed over the best available path based on real-time performance metrics. This adaptive behavior enhances end-to-end QoS by ensuring that traffic always takes the route that best matches its performance requirements.

Wireless networks represent the final mile in many end-to-end QoS strategies. Here, factors such as signal strength, interference, client density, and device capabilities impact performance. Wireless QoS is governed by standards such as Wi-Fi Multimedia, which classifies traffic into access categories with different contention parameters. Access points must map DSCP or CoS markings to the appropriate wireless queues and prioritize real-time traffic such as voice or video. Airtime fairness, client steering, and load balancing further contribute to maintaining QoS in high-density wireless environments. Consistent QoS treatment between wired and wireless domains ensures that applications retain their performance characteristics regardless of how users are connected.

Monitoring and feedback mechanisms are essential to validate and maintain end-to-end QoS. Network telemetry, flow records, SNMP, and performance monitoring tools provide visibility into how traffic is being classified, queued, and forwarded at each hop. Metrics such as latency, jitter, packet loss, and bandwidth utilization must be collected and analyzed in real time to detect bottlenecks or policy violations. When discrepancies are identified, policies can be adjusted to better align with traffic behavior and application needs. Dynamic policy adaptation based on analytics and machine learning represents a new frontier in QoS, allowing the network to automatically tune itself to maintain optimal performance.

Security and QoS also intersect in end-to-end strategies. Firewalls, proxies, and inspection devices must be capable of maintaining or reapplying QoS markings after inspection. Encrypted traffic, particularly with the widespread use of TLS and VPNs, presents a challenge for traditional classification methods. Advanced techniques such as flow metadata analysis and integration with identity-based access controls enable secure yet QoS-aware traffic handling.

Consistency across secure and unencrypted paths is essential to avoid degrading user experience or undermining business-critical applications.

End-to-end QoS strategies are not static configurations but dynamic systems that must evolve with the network. As organizations adopt new applications, cloud services, remote work models, and IoT deployments, the complexity of maintaining consistent QoS increases. The network must support not only traditional voice and data but also virtual reality, video analytics, remote desktops, and real-time telemetry. Each of these services places unique demands on the network, requiring specific combinations of low latency, high bandwidth, minimal jitter, or reliable delivery. End-to-end QoS strategies provide the framework to meet these demands holistically, ensuring that every packet receives the treatment it needs from origin to destination. By coordinating QoS policies across domains, technologies, and vendors, organizations can deliver predictable performance, enforce business priorities, and provide an optimal experience for all users and applications, regardless of where they are or how they connect.

Chapter 37: Implementing QoS on Cisco Devices

Implementing Quality of Service on Cisco devices is a critical practice for ensuring that network traffic is managed according to organizational priorities, application requirements, and performance expectations. Cisco offers one of the most comprehensive and flexible sets of QoS features across its portfolio of routers, switches, firewalls, and wireless controllers. These features allow network administrators to classify, mark, queue, shape, and police traffic at various points in the network. Successful implementation of QoS on Cisco infrastructure requires an understanding of both the theoretical principles of QoS and the specific configuration tools and syntax used on Cisco platforms. Whether in a small branch router or a large data center switch, Cisco's Modular QoS Command-Line Interface provides a consistent and powerful way to apply QoS policies that scale across diverse environments.

The first step in implementing QoS on Cisco devices involves traffic classification. Classification defines which packets belong to which traffic classes, such as voice, video, transactional data, or best-effort traffic. On Cisco devices, classification is typically performed using class maps, which allow administrators to match packets based on various criteria, including IP addresses, protocol types, port numbers, access lists, or DSCP values. For instance, a class map can be created to match all packets with a DSCP value of EF, which corresponds to expedited forwarding and is often used for voice traffic. Once classified, packets can be marked or mapped to queues that reflect their priority.

After classification, the next step is to define how traffic should be treated using policy maps. A policy map references one or more class maps and specifies the QoS actions that should be taken on the traffic within each class. These actions may include setting a new DSCP or CoS value, applying bandwidth guarantees, configuring shaping or policing rates, and assigning packets to specific queues. For example, within a policy map, the voice class might be configured with strict priority queuing, ensuring that it is always serviced ahead of other traffic, while the video class may be assigned a guaranteed bandwidth value and placed in a weighted queue. The best-effort class might simply be allowed to use remaining bandwidth with no special treatment.

Once the policy map is defined, it must be applied to an interface using a service policy. Cisco allows QoS policies to be applied on either the inbound or outbound direction of an interface, depending on where the traffic needs to be controlled. On WAN interfaces, outbound policies are commonly used to manage traffic before it leaves the device, preventing congestion at the provider edge. On access layer switches, inbound policies may be used to classify and mark traffic as it enters the network, ensuring that internal policies are maintained throughout the network path. Cisco devices support hierarchical QoS as well, which allows for nested policy maps that provide even greater granularity and control.

Cisco's implementation of queuing mechanisms is another cornerstone of its QoS strategy. Devices support multiple queuing models, including priority queuing, class-based weighted fair queuing, and low-latency queuing. For example, on WAN routers, low-latency queuing can be used to place voice packets into a strict priority queue with bandwidth policing, while other classes use class-based weighted fair queuing to share the remaining bandwidth fairly. On switches, particularly those in the Catalyst family, hardware-based queuing is used, with queues and buffers managed in the switch ASICs. These switches support advanced features such as Weighted Round Robin scheduling and egress queue shaping, allowing for precise control over how traffic is transmitted from each port.

Cisco switches also use differentiated services code point trust states to determine how incoming packets are treated. By default, many access ports may not trust incoming CoS or DSCP markings from endpoints. Administrators can configure interfaces to trust these values if the endpoints are known to mark traffic correctly, such as with IP phones or video endpoints. Trust boundaries are a critical element in maintaining QoS consistency and preventing rogue devices from marking all of their traffic as high priority. If trust is not configured properly, legitimate real-time traffic might be misclassified and deprioritized, degrading the user experience.

Another essential component of implementing QoS on Cisco devices is congestion management. Devices use mechanisms such as Weighted Random Early Detection to preemptively drop packets from lower-priority queues when buffer thresholds are exceeded. This prevents global synchronization and helps preserve bandwidth for higher-priority traffic during congestion. On WAN links, where bandwidth is limited, traffic shaping can be configured to ensure a steady transmission rate, reducing burstiness and avoiding buffer overruns. Cisco devices also support traffic policing, which allows administrators to enforce hard rate limits on certain classes of traffic. Policers can drop excess packets or mark them with a lower DSCP value for deprioritized handling further downstream.

Cisco platforms often include additional QoS features tailored to specific use cases. For example, in wireless networks managed by Cisco Wireless LAN Controllers, QoS is implemented using profiles that map

DSCP values to WMM access categories. Voice traffic can be prioritized on both the wired and wireless segments of the network, ensuring end-to-end QoS consistency. In MPLS environments, Cisco supports mapping DSCP values to MPLS experimental bits, allowing QoS to extend across the provider core using traffic engineering and class-of-service policies. For cloud connectivity, Cisco SD-WAN solutions provide centralized QoS policy definition and enforcement across a fabric of branch and data center devices, with real-time path selection based on application performance metrics.

Monitoring and validation are critical to maintaining effective QoS policies on Cisco devices. Tools such as Cisco's Embedded Event Manager, Flexible NetFlow, and IP SLA can be used to collect performance data and generate alerts when QoS thresholds are not met. Interfaces provide counters for dropped packets, queue depths, and bandwidth usage per class, allowing administrators to verify that policies are functioning as expected. Cisco DNA Center and other orchestration platforms can provide a graphical interface for defining QoS policies and reviewing their effectiveness across the entire network. By using telemetry and analytics, administrators can refine QoS settings, troubleshoot issues, and ensure continuous alignment with business priorities.

Implementing QoS on Cisco devices is a robust and scalable way to ensure that applications receive the network performance they require. Through a combination of classification, marking, queuing, shaping, and monitoring, administrators can build a network that supports voice, video, data, and cloud services with the reliability and consistency users expect. With a vast array of features, flexible configuration options, and powerful management tools, Cisco's QoS framework provides the foundation for predictable, efficient, and business-aligned network operation across the enterprise.

Chapter 38: Implementing QoS on Juniper Networks

Implementing Quality of Service on Juniper Networks devices involves a powerful and modular approach to managing traffic flows across enterprise, service provider, and data center environments. Juniper's QoS architecture is highly flexible and leverages the robust capabilities of Junos OS, its foundational operating system. Through class-of-service configurations, administrators can prioritize delay-sensitive traffic, enforce bandwidth guarantees, manage congestion, and ensure that mission-critical applications receive preferential treatment across multiple network domains. The QoS mechanisms in Juniper devices are built on a well-defined structure of classifiers, schedulers, shaping policies, and rewrite rules that enable comprehensive traffic control from ingress to egress.

The implementation of QoS in Juniper begins with traffic classification, which is the process of identifying packets and assigning them to forwarding classes. This is typically done by examining specific fields in the packet header, such as IP precedence, DSCP, MPLS EXP bits, or IEEE 802.1p CoS values. Juniper devices use classifiers to map these fields to internal forwarding classes and loss priority levels. A classifier is a set of rules that determine which forwarding class a packet belongs to, based on its markings or other matching criteria. These forwarding classes are then used to control the treatment of the packet throughout the rest of the QoS process.

Once traffic is classified, it is mapped to a forwarding class and assigned a loss priority. Junos supports multiple forwarding classes, and each class can be configured to receive different scheduling, queuing, and drop behavior. The loss priority further refines traffic handling by indicating how likely a packet is to be discarded under congestion conditions. For example, within a single forwarding class, packets with a higher loss priority may be dropped before packets with a lower priority if queues become congested. This dual-tiered classification system gives administrators precise control over how different types of traffic are handled under both normal and stressed network conditions.

Scheduling is the next key component of Juniper's QoS framework. Scheduling defines how packets from different forwarding classes are dequeued and transmitted from the router or switch. Each scheduler defines a transmission rate, buffer size, and priority level. These schedulers are assigned to output queues associated with specific forwarding classes. Junos allows schedulers to be configured using strict-priority, weighted round-robin, or deficit round-robin methods. A strict-priority scheduler ensures that real-time traffic, such as voice, is always sent before any lower-priority traffic. Weighted round-robin and deficit round-robin enable fair bandwidth sharing between classes while honoring their relative importance.

In addition to schedulers, Juniper supports shaping policies that smooth traffic flows and prevent bursts from overwhelming downstream devices. Shaping is typically applied at the interface level and can be used to limit the output rate of traffic from a specific class or the entire interface. By buffering packets and transmitting them at a steady rate, shaping helps maintain predictable latency and reduces the chance of packet drops due to sudden congestion. Shaping is especially important on WAN interfaces or in data centers where oversubscription can lead to performance degradation. Junos allows shaping rates to be defined in bits per second and supports hierarchical shaping for complex multi-tenant environments.

Rewrite rules in Junos are used to modify packet markings at the ingress or egress point of a device. This allows administrators to enforce trust boundaries and ensure consistent QoS markings across different segments of the network. For example, if a packet enters the network with an incorrect DSCP value, a rewrite rule can be used to change it to the correct value based on the forwarding class. Rewrite rules are also used to map internal forwarding class values back to DSCP or EXP bits before the packet is forwarded to the next hop. This is critical in multi-vendor environments where interoperability and marking consistency are essential for end-to-end QoS enforcement.

Juniper's configuration model for QoS is structured and hierarchical, which makes it easier to manage policies across multiple devices and interfaces. Classifiers, forwarding classes, schedulers, and rewrite rules are all defined in separate configuration stanzas and then referenced within the interface configuration. This modularity allows policies to be reused and adapted without duplicating configurations. For example, a single scheduler map can be applied to multiple interfaces, ensuring consistent traffic handling policies throughout the network. This approach reduces configuration errors and simplifies the task of updating QoS policies as network requirements evolve.

Monitoring and visibility are integral to the success of QoS implementation on Juniper devices. Junos provides a variety of operational commands and telemetry options that allow administrators to inspect queue depths, packet counters, drop rates, and buffer utilization. Commands such as show class-of-service interface, show interfaces queue, and monitor interface traffic provide real-time insights into how traffic is being handled. These tools help verify that QoS policies are functioning as intended and support proactive troubleshooting when performance issues arise. For large-scale environments, Juniper also supports integration with network analytics platforms and telemetry streaming, which can provide a comprehensive view of QoS metrics across the entire network fabric.

One of the advantages of Juniper's QoS architecture is its support for scale and high-performance environments. The company's MX series routers, QFX switches, and SRX firewalls are all equipped to handle QoS at line rate, with deep buffer management and hardware-assisted queuing. This makes them well-suited for service provider networks, cloud data centers, and enterprise backbones where QoS policies must be enforced at high throughput with minimal latency overhead. Additionally, Juniper's support for MPLS and segment routing allows QoS to be extended across label-switched paths, ensuring that service levels are maintained even across provider core networks.

QoS implementation on Juniper Networks is not limited to the data plane. Control plane and management traffic can also be classified and prioritized to ensure stable and responsive device operation. Junos allows system-level traffic such as routing updates, ARP, or NTP to be assigned to specific queues and treated with higher priority than general data traffic. This helps maintain network stability and responsiveness even during periods of high load or potential attack scenarios.

Implementing QoS on Juniper Networks devices empowers organizations to deliver reliable, high-performance networking experiences across a wide range of use cases. Whether ensuring voice quality, supporting latency-sensitive applications, or enforcing service-level agreements in a multi-tenant cloud environment, Juniper's class-of-service framework provides the tools needed to build intelligent and responsive networks. Through consistent classification, precise scheduling, adaptive shaping, and real-time monitoring, administrators gain the control necessary to optimize traffic flows and align network behavior with business priorities. The modular design and powerful telemetry capabilities of Junos further enhance the ability to maintain, scale, and evolve QoS policies in step with growing demands and evolving technologies.

Chapter 39: QoS in SD-WAN Solutions

Quality of Service in Software-Defined Wide Area Network solutions represents a transformative shift in how enterprises manage application performance, prioritize network traffic, and optimize resource usage across multiple transport links. Traditional WAN architectures relied heavily on static routing, rigid MPLS circuits, and device-centric QoS policies that were often difficult to scale and complex to manage. In contrast, SD-WAN introduces a dynamic, application-aware, and policy-driven approach to traffic management that integrates QoS as a core function of the architecture. This evolution enables organizations to deliver reliable performance for critical applications across hybrid networks that include broadband internet, LTE, and private circuits, all while reducing costs and improving agility.

At the heart of QoS in SD-WAN is the concept of centralized policy control combined with distributed enforcement. Unlike traditional WANs, where QoS policies are configured manually on individual routers, SD-WAN allows administrators to define policies from a central controller or orchestrator. These policies are then automatically pushed to all edge devices, ensuring consistency and reducing operational overhead. Centralized management simplifies the definition of business intent, allowing policies to reflect application priority, user identity, location, or time of day. For example, a policy can specify that voice and video conferencing traffic must be prioritized across all branches, while software updates and backups should be limited to non-peak hours or relegated to lower-quality links.

Application identification and classification are foundational to effective QoS in SD-WAN. Modern SD-WAN solutions use deep packet inspection, heuristics, and machine learning to accurately identify thousands of applications in real time. This granular visibility enables fine-tuned traffic classification that goes beyond port-based or IP-based matching. Applications are categorized by type, behavior, and performance sensitivity. Critical applications such as VoIP, ERP systems, or virtual desktop sessions are automatically recognized and assigned to high-priority queues, while recreational or bulk traffic like streaming video, file transfers, or social media is placed into lower-priority classes. This classification process occurs at the edge, where traffic first enters the SD-WAN fabric, ensuring that prioritization begins immediately.

Once traffic is classified, SD-WAN devices apply QoS policies to determine how that traffic is queued, shaped, and forwarded across available links. Queuing mechanisms ensure that high-priority traffic is transmitted first, while weighted fair queuing and bandwidth reservation techniques distribute remaining capacity among other traffic classes. Many SD-WAN platforms support low latency queuing for real-time applications, combined with congestion avoidance algorithms that protect interactive flows during periods of high utilization. These queuing and scheduling decisions are performed locally at the edge devices but follow the policies defined centrally, allowing for scalable and consistent enforcement across the network.

A key differentiator of SD-WAN QoS is its ability to leverage path selection based on real-time link performance metrics. Traditional QoS could only optimize traffic on a given link, whereas SD-WAN can choose the best path for each flow across multiple links with varying characteristics. Metrics such as latency, jitter, packet loss, and throughput are continuously monitored for each path, enabling dynamic steering of traffic. For example, if a broadband internet link begins to experience high latency or packet loss, VoIP traffic can be redirected in real time to an MPLS link or LTE backup with better performance characteristics. This application-aware routing enhances the effectiveness of QoS by ensuring that traffic not only receives the correct treatment but also traverses the optimal path.

Another important aspect of QoS in SD-WAN is traffic shaping and policing. Shaping ensures that outbound traffic conforms to defined rate limits, preventing congestion and packet drops at upstream interfaces. This is especially valuable on internet links or wireless connections, where bandwidth availability may vary or be oversubscribed. Policing, on the other hand, enforces strict limits on traffic rates, dropping or re-marking packets that exceed the configured thresholds. While shaping is typically preferred for delay-sensitive traffic, policing may be used to enforce fair usage policies or to limit non-critical applications. Both techniques are integral to maintaining predictable performance in shared environments.

SD-WAN also allows for hierarchical QoS, where multiple layers of traffic classification and treatment are applied. At the first level, traffic is grouped into broad categories such as voice, video, business applications, and best effort. Within each category, further differentiation can be made based on user roles, device types, or departments. For example, executive video conferencing traffic may receive higher priority than general employee video calls, even though both are classified as video. Hierarchical policies enable fine-grained control and ensure that the most important services always receive preferential treatment without starving other applications.

Visibility and analytics are core to sustaining QoS in SD-WAN environments. Most platforms provide detailed dashboards and reports that show application performance, link usage, and policy effectiveness. Administrators can drill down into specific sessions to see how QoS policies impacted latency, jitter, and loss. Alerts can be configured to notify administrators when performance thresholds are breached, triggering policy changes or path adjustments. This feedback loop enables continuous optimization and rapid troubleshooting. Some SD-WAN solutions even incorporate machine learning to suggest policy improvements or automatically adjust settings based on historical usage patterns and emerging trends.

Security is closely tied to QoS in SD-WAN architectures. Encrypted tunnels, firewall policies, and segmentation must coexist with traffic prioritization mechanisms. Modern SD-WAN platforms ensure that QoS markings are preserved even within secure tunnels, enabling consistent treatment across the network. Additionally, traffic inspection and security enforcement are often integrated into the data path, allowing policies to consider both security posture and performance requirements. For example, traffic from unknown or non-compliant devices may be assigned a lower QoS priority, while trusted applications are fast-tracked through secure inspection points.

One of the strengths of SD-WAN QoS is its adaptability to changing network conditions and business requirements. As new applications are deployed or as traffic patterns evolve, policies can be updated centrally and pushed to all locations within minutes. During network failures or maintenance events, the system automatically reroutes traffic and rebalances load across available paths. This dynamic behavior ensures that critical services remain available and performant, even in the face of disruptions. The combination of real-time intelligence, centralized control, and distributed enforcement allows SD-WAN QoS to deliver performance guarantees that traditional WAN models could not achieve.

In multi-cloud and hybrid cloud environments, SD-WAN QoS extends performance optimization beyond the enterprise perimeter. Direct internet access, secure gateways, and cloud on-ramp services are integrated into the SD-WAN fabric, enabling policy-based routing to SaaS and IaaS providers. QoS policies are applied to these cloud-bound flows just like any other traffic, ensuring that users receive a consistent experience whether they are accessing applications in a data center, on a public cloud, or across the internet. This end-to-end approach to QoS is crucial as enterprises continue to decentralize IT services and support remote workforces across the globe.

QoS in SD-WAN solutions marks a significant advancement in network traffic management. It combines the foundational principles of classification, marking, queuing, and shaping with the power of centralized orchestration, real-time path selection, and application awareness. This integrated model allows enterprises to align network behavior with business priorities, maximize the value of diverse transport links, and deliver consistent performance for all users and applications. As networks become more dynamic and application-centric, SD-WAN QoS provides the agility, visibility, and control needed to meet the growing demands of the digital enterprise.

Chapter 40: Monitoring QoS with SNMP and NetFlow

Monitoring Quality of Service implementations is a vital component of maintaining application performance and network reliability. Without proper visibility into how traffic is classified, prioritized, and forwarded, QoS policies can become ineffective or even counterproductive. Two of the most widely used technologies for monitoring QoS in enterprise and service provider environments are the Simple Network Management Protocol (SNMP) and NetFlow. These tools provide administrators with real-time and historical data about traffic patterns, queue utilization, policy effectiveness, and network health. By leveraging SNMP and NetFlow together, organizations can gain a comprehensive view of how their QoS strategies are functioning and make informed decisions about tuning, troubleshooting, and capacity planning.

SNMP is a protocol used to collect data from network devices such as routers, switches, and firewalls. It operates by querying Management Information Base (MIB) variables that are exposed by the devices' operating systems. These variables include interface statistics, error counts, buffer utilization, and queue depths, all of which are critical for evaluating QoS performance. In the context of QoS, SNMP allows administrators to monitor class-based statistics such as the number of packets transmitted or dropped per queue, the amount of bandwidth used by each class of traffic, and whether specific queues are being overutilized or starved. This level of insight is essential for determining if traffic is being correctly prioritized and if the configured policies are aligning with real-world usage patterns.

SNMP-based monitoring tools typically present this data in the form of graphs and dashboards, allowing network engineers to visualize trends over time. For example, if a voice queue is consistently experiencing high drop rates, SNMP statistics can reveal whether the problem is due to oversubscription, misclassification, or insufficient bandwidth allocation. These insights help in refining QoS policies to better accommodate current traffic loads. Additionally, SNMP can be used to generate alerts based on thresholds, notifying administrators when queue usage exceeds acceptable limits or when specific classes of service are underperforming. This proactive alerting allows teams to address issues before they impact end-user experience.

NetFlow complements SNMP by providing detailed flow-level information about the traffic traversing a network. Originally developed by Cisco and now widely supported by other vendors through variants like sFlow and IPFIX, NetFlow captures metadata about each flow, including source and destination IP addresses, ports, protocols, and the volume of traffic exchanged. More importantly for QoS monitoring, NetFlow can include the Differentiated Services Code Point (DSCP) marking for each flow, revealing how traffic is classified and whether QoS policies are being enforced properly. This visibility allows administrators to correlate application performance with QoS behavior and identify anomalies that SNMP counters alone cannot expose.

By analyzing NetFlow data, network teams can determine which applications are consuming the most bandwidth, which users are generating the most traffic, and how traffic is being treated across different paths. For instance, if business-critical applications are marked correctly but are not receiving the expected performance, NetFlow can help identify if they are being routed over suboptimal links or if congestion is occurring elsewhere in the network. It also assists in capacity planning by showing usage trends and helping to predict when additional bandwidth or policy adjustments will be necessary. With this level of detail, QoS management becomes more data-driven and responsive to actual network conditions.

In multi-site and cloud-connected environments, NetFlow provides a critical lens into distributed traffic patterns. As more organizations adopt SD-WAN and hybrid cloud architectures, understanding how QoS is being applied across different transport links becomes more complex. NetFlow exports from branch routers, data center gateways, and cloud on-ramps allow centralized monitoring platforms to aggregate and analyze data from across the entire enterprise network. This unified view ensures that QoS policies are effective not just within a single location but across the broader infrastructure. It also supports regulatory compliance and reporting by documenting how traffic is handled and prioritized over time.

Integration between SNMP and NetFlow is where the true power of QoS monitoring is realized. SNMP provides a high-level view of device and queue performance, while NetFlow offers granular insight into individual flows and application behavior. When used together, these tools enable correlation between device-level performance and application-level experience. For example, SNMP may reveal that a video queue is experiencing congestion, while NetFlow data can identify the specific application or user responsible for the traffic spike. This combined insight supports more accurate troubleshooting and ensures that corrective actions are targeted and effective.

Modern network monitoring platforms often consolidate SNMP and NetFlow data into a single dashboard, applying machine learning and analytics to detect patterns, anomalies, and performance degradation. These platforms can automatically adjust thresholds based on normal behavior, highlight QoS policy violations, and suggest optimizations based on real usage. For instance, if certain applications are consistently marked with best-effort but are critical to business operations, the system might recommend reclassifying them into a higher-priority queue. Similarly, if a QoS queue is underutilized, resources might be reallocated to improve overall efficiency.

Monitoring QoS with SNMP and NetFlow also supports strategic initiatives such as digital transformation, cloud migration, and remote work. As applications become more distributed and user expectations rise, the network must deliver consistent and predictable performance regardless of location. SNMP and NetFlow help organizations validate that their QoS policies are meeting these expectations, identify where improvements are needed, and ensure that investments in infrastructure are yielding the desired outcomes. They also provide the documentation and metrics needed for service-level agreement enforcement, capacity management, and long-term planning.

QoS monitoring is not a one-time task but an ongoing process that evolves with the network. Traffic patterns change, applications are updated, user behavior shifts, and new services are deployed. By continuously collecting and analyzing SNMP and NetFlow data, network teams can adapt their QoS strategies in real time and maintain optimal performance. Whether the goal is to support high-quality voice calls, ensure smooth video conferencing, prioritize business-critical applications, or prevent abuse of network resources, SNMP and NetFlow provide the insight and control necessary to make informed decisions.

With the continued convergence of security, performance, and user experience, QoS monitoring takes on an even greater significance. SNMP and NetFlow allow for contextual analysis, enabling security and operations teams to collaborate on identifying threats, enforcing policy, and maintaining performance. The integration of QoS monitoring into broader network and security operations centers ensures that all aspects of traffic management are aligned with business objectives. In an era where network performance directly impacts productivity, customer satisfaction, and revenue, the ability to monitor and fine-tune QoS using SNMP and NetFlow is not just a best practice—it is a critical capability.

Chapter 41: Troubleshooting QoS Issues

Troubleshooting Quality of Service issues is a critical skill for network engineers tasked with ensuring the consistent performance of applications across increasingly complex and dynamic networks. QoS is designed to manage traffic flows by classifying, prioritizing, marking, queuing, policing, and shaping packets as they traverse the network. However, when QoS is not functioning as expected, users may experience poor voice quality, video jitter, application slowness, or complete service interruptions. Identifying and resolving QoS issues requires a methodical approach, deep understanding of QoS mechanisms, and a clear view into the network path from source to destination. Because QoS operates across multiple layers and devices, any misconfiguration or mismatch at one point in the network can have far-reaching consequences.

The first step in troubleshooting QoS problems is to clearly identify the symptom being reported. It is essential to determine whether the issue is latency, jitter, packet loss, or throughput degradation. Understanding which specific applications or traffic types are affected will help narrow down the investigation. For example, voice quality problems might indicate issues with priority queuing or excessive jitter, while video buffering might suggest problems with bandwidth guarantees or path selection. Once the symptom is clearly defined, the next step is to trace the traffic path end to end, identifying all devices that handle the traffic, including access switches, core routers, firewalls, WAN edge devices, and even cloud gateways if applicable.

One of the most common causes of QoS failure is incorrect or inconsistent classification. If traffic is not properly identified and assigned to the correct class of service at the point of ingress, it will not receive the appropriate treatment downstream. Administrators must verify that the classification rules are correctly matching the intended traffic and that the correct DSCP or CoS values are being applied. This may involve inspecting class maps, access control lists, or deep packet inspection configurations. Additionally, it is important to verify whether the devices trust the markings received or reclassify packets based on their own policies. Trust boundaries must be carefully controlled to prevent misclassification by endpoints or unauthorized devices.

After classification, packet marking must be preserved throughout the network. A frequent issue occurs when intermediate devices strip or overwrite DSCP markings, resulting in traffic being treated as best-effort even if it was originally classified as high priority. Troubleshooting this requires packet captures and inspection at multiple points in the path to verify that markings are intact. Devices like firewalls, load balancers, and NAT gateways are common culprits for remarking or resetting QoS fields. When packet marking is lost or altered, it must be determined whether this behavior is intentional, due to a security policy, or a misconfiguration that needs to be corrected.

Queuing and scheduling problems are another common source of QoS issues. Each network device typically implements a set of hardware or software queues that correspond to different classes of service. If the device does not correctly map incoming packets to these queues, or if the scheduling policy is misconfigured, packets may be delayed or dropped. This is particularly critical for real-time traffic like voice and video, which must be placed in low-latency or strict-priority queues. Administrators should review queuing policies to ensure that traffic is being enqueued as expected and that bandwidth allocations match the intended QoS design. Command-line tools and SNMP counters can be used to check queue utilization, drop rates, and transmission behavior.

Another key area of focus is policing and shaping. Traffic policers drop or remark packets that exceed a defined rate, which can lead to service degradation if thresholds are set too low. Shapers, on the other hand, buffer excess traffic to smooth bursts, but if buffers fill up, drops can still occur. Troubleshooting these mechanisms requires examining policy maps, verifying committed information rates, and reviewing historical traffic patterns to determine whether actual usage is exceeding policy limits. In some cases, shaping policies may not account for packet overhead or protocol behavior, leading to unexpected drops. Adjusting burst sizes, fine-tuning token bucket parameters, and aligning shaping rates with actual link capacity can help resolve these problems.

Path inconsistencies can also cause QoS problems, particularly in networks that use multiple transport methods such as SD-WAN. If different paths offer varying levels of performance or do not enforce the same QoS policies, application performance may be erratic. It is important to ensure that QoS policies are consistent across all paths and that routing or path selection mechanisms account for QoS requirements. Some SD-WAN solutions use real-time link metrics to steer traffic, but if these measurements are inaccurate or thresholds are misconfigured, high-priority traffic may end up on degraded links. Monitoring tools that correlate application performance with path usage can provide insight into these scenarios.

Visibility tools like NetFlow, sFlow, and IPFIX are invaluable for understanding which traffic types are traversing the network and how they are being marked. These tools can reveal whether business-critical applications are receiving the correct treatment or being misclassified. Combining flow visibility with SNMP metrics from interfaces and queues allows administrators to correlate traffic behavior with device-level performance. Packet captures taken at strategic points along the path can validate the presence and integrity of QoS markings, detect delays introduced by queues, and identify packet drops due to shaping or congestion.

Another area to investigate is device performance and resource utilization. QoS processing can be hardware-assisted or software-based depending on the platform and traffic load. If devices are experiencing high CPU utilization or memory exhaustion, QoS functions may not perform reliably. This is particularly important on lower-end switches or routers that may not support advanced QoS features at full line rate. Reviewing device logs, CPU usage, and platform-specific counters can uncover whether resource limitations are affecting QoS enforcement.

Changes in application behavior or network topology can also impact QoS unexpectedly. An application update may change how it communicates, using different ports or protocols that bypass existing classification rules. Network changes, such as adding new links, replacing hardware, or modifying routing paths, can introduce inconsistencies in QoS policies. Change control and documentation are essential to maintaining QoS effectiveness. Administrators should validate QoS configurations after any network change to ensure continued alignment with performance objectives.

In complex environments, cross-functional collaboration is often necessary to troubleshoot QoS issues effectively. Network teams may need to work closely with application developers, security teams, and service providers to trace traffic flows, validate markings, and interpret performance metrics. Escalating to vendor support may be necessary when dealing with platform-specific behavior or bugs. Successful QoS troubleshooting requires not only technical expertise but also a structured process, comprehensive monitoring, and the ability to see the big picture across all layers of the network stack. By identifying the root cause and making targeted adjustments, administrators can restore service quality, prevent recurrence, and strengthen the overall reliability of their QoS strategy.

Chapter 42: Simulating QoS Scenarios

Simulating Quality of Service scenarios is a valuable technique for understanding the behavior of network policies under various conditions and for validating QoS configurations before deploying them in production. By recreating realistic traffic patterns and network environments in a controlled setting, engineers can observe how different classes of traffic are prioritized, how queuing and scheduling mechanisms respond to congestion, and how shaping and policing policies affect performance. Simulation helps identify potential misconfigurations, fine-tune QoS parameters, and ensure that business-critical applications receive the service levels they require. It also allows for training, experimentation, and proactive planning in a risk-free environment, where performance can be analyzed without impacting live systems.

Creating a QoS simulation environment involves setting up a testbed that includes the necessary networking hardware or virtual devices, along with traffic generators and monitoring tools. The testbed should mimic the structure of the production network, including access, distribution, and core layers if possible. It should include multiple types of traffic flows such as voice, video, transactional data, web browsing, and background file transfers. Each traffic type should be clearly defined with its own characteristics in terms of bandwidth usage, latency sensitivity, jitter tolerance, and burstiness. This diversity allows the simulation to reflect real-world conditions where multiple applications compete for limited resources.

Traffic generation is a critical component of QoS simulation. Specialized tools such as Ixia, Spirent, Ostinato, and open-source options like iPerf or D-ITG can be used to create synthetic traffic that mimics the behavior of real applications. These tools allow administrators to control variables such as packet size, flow rate, protocol type, and duration. For example, voice traffic can be simulated with a consistent stream of small UDP packets at fixed intervals, while video streams can be emulated with variable bit rate flows that fluctuate over time. Background traffic can be created with large TCP transfers to stress the network and induce congestion. By generating different traffic mixes, engineers can evaluate how well QoS mechanisms protect high-priority traffic under load.

In the simulation, classification and marking policies should be applied at the ingress points, just as they would be in a production network. These policies must correctly identify traffic types and assign appropriate QoS markings, such as DSCP values or MPLS EXP bits. The markings must then be honored and interpreted consistently by all downstream devices. Simulating scenarios where markings are incorrect or missing helps assess the impact of misclassification and validates whether re-marking policies are effective. It also demonstrates the importance of trust boundaries and the need for careful control over which devices are allowed to mark traffic.

Once traffic is flowing through the testbed, the focus shifts to observing how queues behave. Devices should be configured with queuing policies such as strict priority queuing, weighted fair queuing, or class-based queuing. Monitoring queue depth, packet drop counts, and transmission latency reveals whether traffic is being forwarded according to its assigned priority. For instance, if real-time voice traffic is delayed or dropped when competing with large data transfers, it may indicate that the priority queue is misconfigured or that bandwidth allocation is insufficient. Engineers can adjust queue weights, buffer sizes, or scheduling algorithms and observe the resulting changes in performance.

Simulating network congestion is one of the most informative scenarios in QoS testing. By intentionally overloading interfaces with traffic, engineers can examine how the network responds when demand exceeds capacity. This includes observing how lower-priority traffic is delayed or dropped, whether shaping policies smooth out traffic bursts, and whether policing correctly limits excessive flows. Congestion scenarios help validate that QoS policies are not only prioritizing critical traffic but also enforcing fairness and protecting the network from misuse. They also test the ability of the network to maintain application performance during peak usage, which is critical for supporting real-time services like voice and video.

Another important simulation involves testing link failures and routing changes. In networks with multiple paths, QoS must remain effective even when traffic is rerouted due to a failure or load-balancing decision. By simulating link loss and failover events, engineers can evaluate whether QoS policies remain consistent across alternate paths and whether backup links provide adequate bandwidth and queuing capabilities. This is particularly important in SD-WAN and hybrid environments where path selection is dynamic and can be influenced by real-time performance metrics. A well-designed QoS policy should be portable across all possible paths and maintain application experience regardless of underlying changes in topology.

Time-based scenarios are also useful in QoS simulation. By scheduling different traffic types at various times of day, engineers can test whether QoS policies adapt to changes in usage patterns. For example, during business hours, the network may prioritize collaboration tools and enterprise applications, while after hours it may allow greater bandwidth for backups or software updates. Simulating these transitions tests the responsiveness and flexibility of the QoS system. It also helps identify whether any residual effects, such as persistent queue buildup or delayed retransmissions, carry over into the next traffic cycle and degrade performance.

Real-time monitoring tools are essential for capturing data during QoS simulations. Packet analyzers like Wireshark can inspect traffic for correct markings and measure latency and jitter. SNMP-based tools can monitor interface and queue statistics, while flow collectors can track traffic volumes and application behavior. Combining these tools provides a multi-dimensional view of network performance and allows for comprehensive analysis of how QoS policies are applied and enforced. Engineers should compare observed metrics against expected performance levels to determine whether QoS objectives are being met and where adjustments may be necessary.

One of the key benefits of simulating QoS scenarios is the opportunity to test edge cases and worst-case conditions. These include high packet loss rates, asymmetric routing, microbursts, and interactions between QoS and security policies such as firewalls and intrusion prevention systems. By exploring these edge scenarios, engineers can uncover hidden dependencies and limitations in their QoS design. For example, a firewall might reset DSCP markings after deep packet inspection, or a VPN tunnel might encapsulate traffic in a way that bypasses QoS classification rules. Identifying and resolving these issues in a simulation environment prevents performance degradation in production and improves overall policy robustness.

Simulating QoS scenarios builds confidence in the design and implementation of network policies. It empowers engineers to make data-driven decisions, improves troubleshooting skills, and provides a clear understanding of how changes in configuration affect application behavior. By investing time in realistic simulation, organizations can deploy QoS with greater assurance that it will perform as expected under a variety of conditions, ultimately supporting a more resilient and efficient network infrastructure.

Chapter 43: QoS Testing and Verification Tools

Quality of Service testing and verification tools play a critical role in validating the effectiveness of QoS policies within a network infrastructure. As networks grow more complex and application demands become more dynamic, simply configuring QoS is not enough. It must be tested, monitored, and verified to ensure that traffic is being classified, prioritized, shaped, and queued correctly according to business and technical requirements. A wide range of tools is available to assist network engineers in validating QoS configurations, observing behavior under load, and verifying that service-level objectives are consistently met. These tools include software utilities, hardware appliances, built-in operating system commands, protocol analyzers, flow collectors, simulation environments, and cloud-based platforms.

Among the most commonly used tools for QoS testing is iPerf, an open-source utility that generates TCP and UDP traffic between two endpoints. iPerf allows engineers to create controlled flows of data that can be used to measure bandwidth, latency, jitter, and packet loss. By marking iPerf traffic with specific DSCP values, testers can observe how the network prioritizes or deprioritizes each flow, and whether those markings are preserved across the network. iPerf can simulate both real-time and bulk traffic, and it is frequently used in conjunction with network performance monitoring to verify the effectiveness of shaping, policing, and queuing configurations. By adjusting traffic rates and packet sizes, iPerf can stress various classes of service and reveal how well the network manages congestion.

Another valuable category of QoS testing tools includes commercial traffic generators such as Spirent TestCenter and Keysight IxNetwork. These appliances and software platforms are capable of simulating thousands of concurrent flows with diverse characteristics. They offer highly granular control over traffic types, QoS markings, and path selection. Unlike basic tools, these platforms also provide sophisticated reporting, automation, and integration with network infrastructure. Spirent and IxNetwork can emulate enterprise or service provider networks, complete with VLAN tagging, MPLS labels, and application-level behavior. These tools are used extensively in pre-deployment validation, benchmarking, and regression testing, where organizations need to verify that network devices perform according to specifications under real-world conditions.

For live network verification, packet analyzers such as Wireshark offer deep insight into how individual packets are treated by the network. Wireshark captures traffic at the bit level, allowing engineers to inspect IP headers, DSCP values, CoS fields, and other QoS-related information. With Wireshark, it is possible to confirm whether classification is correct, whether DSCP values are being preserved or altered, and whether traffic is being forwarded as expected. By analyzing timestamped traffic flows, engineers can calculate one-way delay, jitter, and out-of-order packets, all of which affect the perceived quality of applications such as VoIP and video. Wireshark's filtering capabilities also help isolate specific classes of traffic for targeted analysis, making it an indispensable tool in both lab and production environments.

SNMP-based monitoring platforms also contribute to QoS verification. Tools like SolarWinds, PRTG, and Cisco Prime Infrastructure collect queue statistics, interface counters, and class-based metrics from routers and switches. These tools enable visualization of queue depth, drop rates, and utilization over time, providing a macro-level view of how QoS policies perform under different traffic conditions. By comparing SNMP-collected data against expected behavior, administrators can identify whether queues are properly sized, whether traffic is classified into the right class, and whether bandwidth guarantees are being honored. Alerts can also be configured to trigger when QoS performance deviates from baseline, supporting proactive troubleshooting and optimization.

Flow-based tools such as NetFlow, sFlow, and IPFIX allow engineers to analyze network traffic patterns and verify QoS treatment at the flow level. Tools like Plixer Scrutinizer, ntopng, and ManageEngine NetFlow Analyzer ingest flow records and display metrics such as top talkers, DSCP usage, application types, and path behaviors. This visibility is crucial for understanding how applications are behaving in the network, whether their traffic is marked appropriately, and whether paths are experiencing congestion. These tools can also correlate performance metrics with QoS policies to confirm whether application SLAs are being met. Flow collectors are particularly effective in multi-site environments where centralized visibility is needed to ensure end-to-end QoS consistency.

In virtualized and cloud environments, QoS verification can be more challenging due to the abstraction of network infrastructure. Tools such as VMware vRealize Network Insight and Microsoft Network Performance Monitor are used to monitor traffic flows in virtual environments, correlating application behavior with underlying QoS policies. These tools provide visibility into virtual switches, tunnel endpoints, and cloud transit paths where traditional SNMP or packet capture tools may not apply. QoS testing in these environments often involves synthetic monitoring tools like ThousandEyes or AppNeta, which simulate user behavior from cloud agents and measure application performance across hybrid paths. These solutions provide a complete picture of how cloud-hosted services perform relative to QoS targets.

Another emerging area of QoS verification involves the use of telemetry and streaming analytics. Platforms such as Cisco DNA Center, Juniper HealthBot, and Arista CloudVision stream real-time performance metrics from network devices using gRPC, JSON, and OpenConfig protocols. These telemetry streams include queue statistics, interface states, drop counters, and latency measurements that can be consumed by analytics engines. By feeding this data into machine learning algorithms or time-series databases like InfluxDB and Grafana, organizations can visualize QoS performance, detect anomalies, and automate responses to emerging issues. This continuous feedback loop enhances the effectiveness of QoS by enabling dynamic policy adjustment based on actual network conditions.

For verification during network changes or after policy updates, synthetic testing tools such as PathSolutions TotalView, NetBrain, and LiveAction are used to simulate traffic behavior and validate routing and QoS policies. These tools often integrate with configuration management systems and can automatically verify that traffic marked for a specific class follows the expected path and receives the correct treatment. Some platforms support rule-based testing, allowing administrators to define expected behavior for specific applications and automatically flag deviations. This capability is especially valuable in environments with frequent changes, such as during mergers, data center migrations, or WAN transformations.

QoS testing and verification tools are not limited to engineers with specialized hardware or extensive budgets. Many open-source and community-supported tools can perform essential QoS tests, especially in smaller networks. Tools like SmokePing can measure latency and jitter across multiple paths, while D-ITG can simulate multimedia traffic and evaluate the impact of congestion. These lightweight tools provide educational and operational value, helping administrators gain hands-on experience with QoS behavior and performance metrics.

Ultimately, the combination of testing and verification tools empowers organizations to move from reactive to proactive QoS management. By continuously validating policies, identifying discrepancies, and refining configurations, network teams can ensure that their QoS strategies are not only in place but are functioning effectively in the face of changing applications, traffic patterns, and user demands. Whether through traffic generation, flow analysis, packet inspection, or synthetic testing, these tools form the foundation of a successful and measurable QoS deployment.

Chapter 44: Security Considerations in QoS

Quality of Service is primarily focused on ensuring that network traffic is classified, prioritized, and delivered according to predefined performance policies. While QoS is designed to optimize traffic flow and support application performance, it is also essential to consider the security implications associated with implementing QoS in enterprise and service provider networks. Failing to account for security when designing and deploying QoS policies can open up vulnerabilities, provide opportunities for abuse, and compromise the integrity of network performance. Security considerations in QoS encompass trust boundaries, policy enforcement, classification integrity, encryption impacts, and the potential for exploitation by malicious users or devices.

One of the most critical security concerns in QoS is the manipulation of packet markings by endpoints. QoS relies on traffic classification, often using fields such as DSCP, IP precedence, or Layer 2 CoS to determine how traffic should be treated. However, these fields can be altered by any device with access to the network unless strict controls are enforced. Without proper trust boundaries, unauthorized users or compromised devices can mark their traffic with high-priority values in an attempt to gain preferential access to network resources. This behavior, often referred to as QoS spoofing, can degrade service for legitimate high-priority traffic and reduce the overall effectiveness of QoS policies.

To mitigate marking abuse, network administrators must clearly define and enforce QoS trust boundaries. These boundaries determine which interfaces or devices are trusted to set QoS markings and which are not. Typically, access-layer devices such as switches and access points are configured to inspect incoming packets and either accept, remark, or drop traffic based on its QoS markings. Untrusted interfaces should reset DSCP or CoS values to defaults or reclassify traffic based on known parameters such as IP address, VLAN, or protocol type. This ensures that only authenticated and authorized traffic is allowed to retain or obtain high-priority status. Trust boundaries should be explicitly defined at every ingress point in the network to prevent unauthorized manipulation of traffic classification.

Another security consideration involves the interaction between QoS policies and traffic inspection devices such as firewalls, intrusion detection systems, and secure web gateways. These devices often operate at Layer 4 or higher and may reassemble traffic flows, decrypt content, or apply policy enforcement based on application signatures. During this inspection process, QoS markings may be removed or modified, either intentionally or as a side effect of the inspection process. If these markings are not preserved or restored after inspection, downstream devices may fail to recognize the priority of the traffic, leading to suboptimal treatment. To maintain QoS effectiveness, security devices must be QoS-aware and capable of reapplying the correct markings based on classification results.

Encryption also poses challenges to QoS, particularly in the context of increasing use of HTTPS, VPNs, and IPsec tunnels. When traffic is encrypted, intermediate devices may be unable to inspect packet payloads or headers beyond the outermost encryption layer. This limits the ability to classify traffic based on application or port, forcing reliance on outer header markings or static policies. In IPsec tunnels, the original QoS markings may be copied to the outer IP header using features such as DSCP preservation, but this behavior must be explicitly enabled and correctly configured. Similarly, QoS policies on VPN concentrators must consider both the encrypted and decrypted states of traffic to ensure consistent policy application.

Malicious actors can also exploit QoS mechanisms to conduct denial-of-service attacks or disrupt service quality for other users. For example, an attacker might generate a large volume of traffic marked as high priority to flood strict-priority queues, causing real-time applications to be dropped or delayed. This type of attack, sometimes called QoS starvation or queue saturation, is especially dangerous in networks that do not implement policing or bandwidth limits on high-priority classes. To protect against such attacks, administrators should apply rate limiting, traffic policing, or shaping on all QoS classes, including those designated for real-time traffic. Priority queues should have maximum bandwidth caps and policies to discard or downgrade excessive traffic.

Misconfiguration is another potential risk area in QoS security. Incorrect class maps, policy maps, or scheduling parameters can inadvertently grant inappropriate priority to non-critical traffic or degrade performance for essential applications. Errors in matching criteria can lead to classification mismatches, where sensitive data is marked for low-priority treatment or bulk transfers receive expedited handling. Configuration verification, change management processes, and automated validation tools can help prevent such errors. Additionally, logging and auditing mechanisms should track QoS policy changes to provide accountability and enable forensics in the event of an incident.

Network segmentation also plays a key role in secure QoS design. By segmenting traffic into separate VLANs, VRFs, or logical interfaces, administrators can isolate traffic types and apply differentiated QoS policies based on security domain. For instance, guest traffic may be assigned to a low-priority queue with strict bandwidth limits, while internal business applications receive guaranteed bandwidth in a separate segment. This not only supports performance but also enforces security boundaries between user groups, departments, or services. In environments with regulatory compliance requirements, such as PCI-DSS or HIPAA, segmentation combined with QoS can ensure that sensitive data is both protected and prioritized appropriately.

The role of identity and access management in QoS security is growing as networks adopt user- and device-aware policies. Modern access control systems can dynamically assign QoS policies based on user roles, authentication status, or endpoint posture. For example, a device that passes a health check may receive higher QoS treatment, while a device lacking security patches may be restricted to a limited service class. These dynamic policies enhance security by aligning QoS privileges with trust levels. Integrating QoS with identity frameworks such as 802.1X, RADIUS, or SAML provides a scalable way to enforce these relationships across distributed networks.

In cloud and hybrid environments, maintaining QoS security becomes even more complex. Traffic traverses multiple domains, including enterprise networks, internet paths, and public cloud infrastructure. Each segment may have different QoS capabilities and enforcement mechanisms, making end-to-end security consistency challenging. Tunneling protocols, encryption, and multi-tenant platforms introduce additional layers of abstraction. To maintain QoS integrity, organizations must collaborate with service providers to understand how markings are handled, how policies are mapped across networks, and how traffic is prioritized within cloud services. Service-level agreements should include QoS guarantees, and traffic verification should be conducted regularly using synthetic monitoring or flow analysis.

Security in QoS is not an afterthought but a foundational requirement for reliable and trustworthy network operations. The same mechanisms that ensure application performance must also protect against abuse, misconfiguration, and exploitation. As networks become more software-defined, policy-driven, and distributed, the integration of security and QoS will only grow more important. Building secure QoS policies requires a combination of technical controls, architectural design, operational discipline, and ongoing monitoring. By treating QoS as both a performance and security function, organizations can ensure not only that critical applications work as expected, but also that the network remains resilient, trustworthy, and aligned with business and compliance goals.

Chapter 45: QoS and Network Virtualization

Quality of Service and network virtualization converge at a crucial intersection in modern network architectures where flexibility, performance, and scalability must coexist. As organizations embrace virtualization to support dynamic workloads, cloud applications, and multi-tenant environments, the traditional methods of QoS enforcement face significant transformation. Network virtualization abstracts physical resources into logical components, allowing for multiple virtual networks to coexist on the same physical infrastructure. This introduces unique challenges and opportunities for QoS because traffic must be prioritized not only within physical links but also across virtual interfaces, overlays, and software-defined components that may span multiple domains.

In virtualized environments, network functions that were once delivered by dedicated hardware devices are now implemented as virtual machines or containers. Routers, firewalls, load balancers, and switches can all be instantiated in software, forming what is commonly referred to as network functions virtualization. These virtual network functions rely on hypervisors, virtual switches, and orchestrators to control data plane behavior. This shift means that QoS policies must now be implemented within these virtual elements rather than on physical devices alone. For example, virtual switches such as VMware vSwitch, Open vSwitch, or those embedded in cloud platforms are responsible for classifying, queuing, and marking packets within a virtualized server environment.

QoS in this context must begin at the virtual network interface of the workload itself. Each virtual machine or container generates traffic that needs to be identified, prioritized, and treated according to policy. Marking traffic at the source is critical for ensuring that QoS intentions are carried throughout the infrastructure. This requires integration with hypervisors and virtual NIC drivers to apply DSCP markings or other classification attributes as traffic exits the workload and enters the virtual switch. In environments with multiple tenants, it becomes necessary to enforce trust boundaries at the virtualization layer, ensuring that one tenant cannot mark all their traffic as high priority and monopolize shared resources.

Once traffic is marked and classified, it traverses the virtual switch where queuing and bandwidth management take place. Virtual switches support a limited number of hardware queues per physical NIC, which must be shared among all virtual ports. This limitation requires intelligent scheduling and shaping policies to ensure that high-priority traffic is not delayed by best-effort or background traffic. Techniques such as rate limiting, minimum bandwidth guarantees, and weighted fair queuing are implemented in the virtual switch to enforce QoS policies. In more advanced configurations, network interface cards that support SR-IOV or DPDK can offload QoS functions to hardware, providing better performance and isolation for virtualized traffic.

Overlay networks further complicate QoS in virtualized environments. Technologies such as VXLAN, GRE, or NVGRE encapsulate packets with additional headers to enable logical network segmentation over shared physical infrastructure. This encapsulation can obscure the original QoS markings, leading to misclassification or loss of priority as the packet traverses the physical underlay network. To preserve QoS across overlays, virtual network infrastructure must be capable of mapping inner markings to outer headers and back again. This process, known as QoS remarking or DSCP tunneling, is essential for maintaining consistent traffic treatment across both virtual and physical network segments.

Cloud environments, whether public or private, introduce another layer of abstraction and complexity. In cloud networks, tenants have limited visibility and control over the physical network infrastructure. As a result, QoS policies must often be enforced at the virtual edge, within the virtual routers and gateways that connect tenant networks to shared services. Cloud providers may offer service classes or bandwidth guarantees, but the mapping between virtual QoS policies and the underlying physical network is opaque to the tenant. This requires careful coordination between application requirements, virtual infrastructure policies, and service-level agreements to ensure that QoS expectations are met.

In multi-tenant environments, QoS becomes a critical tool for resource fairness and performance isolation. Each tenant may have its own set of applications, users, and priorities. Without proper QoS enforcement, one tenant could consume excessive bandwidth, degrade latency-sensitive traffic, or cause jitter for other tenants sharing the same infrastructure. Virtualized QoS policies must therefore include per-tenant shaping, class-based queuing, and policing mechanisms to enforce usage limits and maintain fairness. This isolation is not only important for performance but also for security and compliance in regulated industries where traffic separation is mandatory.

Software-defined networking plays a central role in managing QoS in virtualized environments. SDN separates the control plane from the data plane, allowing centralized controllers to define and push QoS policies across distributed virtual and physical elements. These controllers have a global view of the network and can dynamically adjust QoS parameters based on real-time conditions, application behavior, or user identity. For example, an SDN controller might detect that a video conferencing application is experiencing increased latency and respond by reconfiguring traffic priorities or steering flows along alternate paths. This level of agility and programmability is essential for maintaining QoS in highly dynamic, virtualized networks.

Monitoring and visibility tools must also evolve to support QoS in virtualized networks. Traditional SNMP and NetFlow tools may not capture traffic within virtual switches or containers. Instead, telemetry from hypervisors, orchestration platforms, and SDN controllers must be collected and analyzed to understand how traffic is being classified, marked, and forwarded. Tools such as VMware vRealize Network Insight, OpenStack Telemetry, or Kubernetes-based observability platforms can provide insights into virtual traffic flows and QoS performance. This visibility is necessary for verifying policy compliance, detecting congestion, and optimizing resource allocation across virtual components.

As workloads move dynamically between hosts, data centers, or cloud regions, QoS policies must follow them. This requires integration between orchestration systems such as OpenStack, Kubernetes, or VMware NSX and the underlying QoS infrastructure. Policies must be applied automatically as workloads are created, moved, or destroyed, ensuring that traffic always receives the intended treatment regardless of location. This dynamic QoS provisioning is essential in environments with high mobility, such as virtual desktop infrastructure, hybrid cloud deployments, or continuous integration pipelines.

Ultimately, integrating QoS with network virtualization demands a deep understanding of both technologies. It is not enough to configure QoS policies at the physical network edge; those policies must extend into the virtual realm, adapt to dynamic workloads, and remain consistent across overlays, hypervisors, and containers. Engineers must think holistically, designing QoS strategies that span virtual and physical boundaries while accounting for the unique behaviors and limitations of each layer. When done correctly, QoS and network virtualization together empower organizations to deliver scalable, efficient, and predictable network services, even in the face of growing complexity and demand.

Chapter 46: QoS for IoT Networks

Quality of Service in Internet of Things networks is increasingly critical as the number of connected devices grows exponentially and their roles in mission-critical applications expand. IoT networks are fundamentally different from traditional enterprise or consumer networks due to their unique characteristics, such as the massive scale of connected endpoints, their diverse traffic patterns, and the varied latency and reliability requirements across device types. Some IoT devices transmit small, periodic updates with minimal bandwidth needs, while others carry out real-time functions that are highly sensitive to delay and jitter. A well-designed QoS framework for IoT networks must be capable of prioritizing traffic based on application context, ensuring reliability for critical functions, and accommodating the constraints of devices and connectivity technologies with limited resources.

In an IoT ecosystem, devices can range from low-power sensors and actuators to industrial controllers, surveillance cameras, medical instruments, and smart appliances. These devices often coexist on the same network infrastructure, generating traffic that varies significantly in volume, timing, and importance. For instance, a temperature sensor may send a reading every few minutes, while a smart security camera may stream high-definition video continuously. At the same time, a manufacturing robot may need sub-millisecond latency to respond to control commands. This diversity necessitates a QoS model that can distinguish between latency-sensitive and best-effort traffic and allocate network resources accordingly. Without proper QoS, critical IoT functions can be disrupted by bandwidth-heavy but less urgent traffic.

The foundation of QoS for IoT begins with accurate traffic classification. Every IoT device or application must be identified based on its purpose, communication pattern, and priority level. Classification can be performed by analyzing traffic headers, port numbers, protocols used, or even device MAC addresses and IP ranges. In industrial environments, protocols such as MQTT, CoAP, Modbus, and OPC UA are commonly used by IoT devices, and recognizing these protocols is essential for assigning the correct QoS treatment. Once classified, traffic can be marked with DSCP or other QoS tags to guide treatment across the network. Markings should reflect the device's operational criticality rather than just the type of traffic, ensuring that a safety alert is always treated with higher priority than a software update or system log.

One of the main challenges in implementing QoS for IoT is the constrained nature of many devices and networks. Many IoT endpoints have limited processing power, memory, and energy resources, which means they cannot perform complex QoS operations themselves. Additionally, many IoT networks use wireless technologies such as Wi-Fi, Zigbee, LoRaWAN, or cellular (including NB-IoT and LTE-M), which have inherently variable performance characteristics. Wireless interference, signal attenuation, and congestion can affect delivery reliability and timing. In such environments, QoS must often be implemented at the gateway or edge device level, where traffic from multiple IoT endpoints converges before entering the broader network. Edge devices must classify, prioritize, and buffer traffic as needed, serving as the primary enforcement point for QoS policies.

Edge computing also plays a key role in supporting QoS for IoT. By processing data locally rather than sending all information to the cloud, edge computing reduces the volume of network traffic and the dependency on long-haul links. This allows bandwidth to be conserved for critical traffic and minimizes the risk of congestion affecting time-sensitive operations. QoS policies at the edge can be dynamically adjusted based on data analytics and real-time performance metrics. For example, an edge node can detect that a temperature sensor is reporting values outside of safe ranges and immediately elevate its traffic priority to ensure timely delivery to the control system. This context-aware prioritization enhances the responsiveness and reliability of IoT networks.

In environments such as smart cities or intelligent transportation systems, IoT traffic spans multiple domains and administrative boundaries. Devices such as traffic lights, environmental monitors, surveillance systems, and public safety devices all transmit data to different applications and stakeholders. QoS policies must be coordinated across these domains to maintain end-to-end performance. For instance, video from a street camera involved in an emergency response must be prioritized from the edge sensor, through the metropolitan network, to the central command center. This requires consistent QoS markings, inter-domain trust models, and possibly service-level agreements with third-party providers. The ability to maintain QoS across heterogeneous infrastructure is critical for IoT deployments that have real-time or safety-critical elements.

Scalability is another key factor when designing QoS for IoT networks. As the number of connected devices grows, the network must handle increasing traffic volumes without compromising service quality. Static QoS configurations that work for small deployments may not scale well when tens or hundreds of thousands of devices are added. Dynamic QoS systems, which can adjust traffic priorities and bandwidth allocations based on current conditions and policies, offer a more sustainable approach. These systems may leverage SDN controllers or orchestration platforms that monitor traffic in real time and automatically update forwarding rules and queue assignments across the network.

Security considerations also intersect with QoS in IoT networks. Devices that are compromised or behave abnormally may attempt to flood the network with high-priority traffic, either by spoofing DSCP markings or by exploiting misconfigurations. QoS policies must include safeguards against such abuse, such as limiting the rate of traffic per device or class, verifying markings at the edge, and employing anomaly detection to identify suspicious patterns. Network segmentation and access control further enhance QoS security by isolating traffic from different device groups and applying differentiated policies based on the device's identity, role, or trust level.

Monitoring and visibility are essential to validate that QoS policies are working effectively in IoT environments. Because of the distributed nature of IoT deployments, traditional monitoring tools may not provide sufficient insight into how traffic is being handled at the edge or across wireless links. Specialized IoT network monitoring tools or extended telemetry from gateways and edge platforms can provide data on packet loss, latency, jitter, and throughput for each class of service. This information supports proactive maintenance, real-time troubleshooting, and continuous optimization of QoS policies based on actual device behavior and performance metrics.

QoS in IoT networks enables not just better performance but also more reliable and resilient operations. By ensuring that mission-critical traffic is prioritized, that network resources are allocated efficiently, and that congestion is minimized, QoS supports the stability and effectiveness of IoT applications across every industry. From smart factories and healthcare systems to utility grids and public safety, the ability to deliver differentiated service treatment ensures that IoT networks can meet the expectations placed upon them as essential components of modern digital infrastructure. A well-implemented QoS strategy provides the foundation for scalable, secure, and responsive IoT deployments capable of supporting the next generation of intelligent systems.

Chapter 47: QoS in Data Center Environments

Quality of Service in data center environments is essential to ensure predictable performance, traffic prioritization, and efficient resource utilization for the vast array of applications and services hosted within these highly dense and mission-critical infrastructures. Unlike enterprise or campus networks, data centers operate at extremely high speeds, often with links reaching 10, 25, 40, or 100 Gbps, and with applications that demand minimal latency, near-zero packet loss, and deterministic throughput. In these settings, QoS mechanisms are not just beneficial but often necessary to support virtual machines, containers, storage traffic, real-time analytics, high-frequency trading applications, backup operations, and internal control traffic that all compete for shared bandwidth.

The data center environment is unique in that it hosts both north-south and east-west traffic. North-south traffic refers to data entering or leaving the data center, typically between end-users and applications. East-west traffic, on the other hand, refers to communications between servers within the data center, such as interactions between microservices, virtual machines, or application tiers. The rise of distributed architectures, such as microservices and container-based deployments, has significantly increased the volume of east-west traffic, making internal network performance just as critical as external connectivity. QoS policies must be carefully designed to handle both types of traffic, ensuring that latency-sensitive workloads are not impacted by bulk transfers or background processes.

A fundamental aspect of QoS in data centers is traffic classification. Accurate classification allows the network to identify the type of traffic and apply appropriate queuing, scheduling, and forwarding policies. Traffic types in data centers often include storage traffic using protocols such as iSCSI or NFS, hypervisor control traffic like vMotion, real-time application flows, and background data replication. Each of these has different performance requirements. For instance, storage traffic must have low jitter and packet loss to avoid throughput degradation, while vMotion requires consistent bandwidth to ensure smooth virtual machine migration. Real-time analytics might require both low latency and guaranteed delivery, whereas backup traffic can tolerate delay but must not be dropped.

Once traffic is classified, marking mechanisms such as Differentiated Services Code Point values or IEEE 802.1p Class of Service bits are applied to indicate the priority of packets. These markings guide how switches and routers handle traffic within the data center. Data center switches, particularly those in the top-of-rack, spine, and core layers, must support deep buffers, low latency, and advanced queuing capabilities to manage large-scale traffic flows without congestion. Lossless Ethernet technologies, such as Data Center Bridging, are often employed to ensure that no packets are dropped for critical traffic classes like storage or HPC workloads. This is achieved through mechanisms such as Priority Flow Control, which pauses traffic on a per-priority basis when congestion is detected, allowing critical flows to continue unimpeded.

Queuing and scheduling are core QoS mechanisms used to manage contention for switch buffers and output interfaces. In data centers, switches typically implement multiple queues per interface, each mapped to a specific traffic class. Scheduling algorithms such as weighted round robin or strict priority determine how packets are dequeued and transmitted. High-priority queues may be serviced more frequently or even exclusively in the case of strict priority scheduling. However, care must be taken to prevent starvation of lower-priority queues, which could lead to application degradation or control plane instability. In environments with highly bursty traffic, buffer tuning and intelligent scheduling are essential to ensure fair access and prevent packet drops.

Shaping and policing mechanisms are also applied in data center QoS strategies. Traffic shaping smooths out bursts by buffering packets and transmitting them at a controlled rate, which is useful for preventing oversubscription on downstream links. This is particularly important for high-volume applications such as database replication or big data processing, where traffic spikes can overwhelm network resources. Policing, on the other hand, enforces strict rate limits by dropping or remarking packets that exceed configured thresholds. While effective for controlling traffic usage, policing can cause performance issues if not carefully configured, especially for TCP-based applications that react negatively to packet loss.

In virtualized data centers, QoS must extend into the virtual network layer. Hypervisors and virtual switches must support QoS policies that prioritize traffic between virtual machines on the same host and across the network. Technologies like VMware vSphere, Microsoft Hyper-V, and KVM provide features for setting bandwidth limits, assigning priority queues, and integrating with physical NICs that support hardware-based QoS enforcement. These capabilities allow for consistent traffic treatment whether it originates from a physical server or a virtualized workload. Container environments, such as those managed by Kubernetes, require similar integration with network plugins and policies that support traffic shaping, policing, and prioritization at the pod or namespace level.

Overlay networks, such as those built using VXLAN, also play a significant role in modern data center QoS. Overlays abstract the physical topology and provide isolation between tenants or applications, but they introduce additional headers that can complicate QoS enforcement. To ensure end-to-end QoS, network devices must be capable of inspecting encapsulated packets and mapping inner markings to outer headers during encapsulation and vice versa during decapsulation. This mapping ensures that traffic retains its priority treatment across the underlay network and that QoS policies are consistent regardless of overlay usage.

Data center interconnects and multi-site environments introduce another layer of complexity. When traffic moves between geographically distributed data centers, QoS policies must be extended across WAN links, often with limited bandwidth compared to intra-data center links. Technologies such as MPLS, SD-WAN, and dedicated interconnects provide mechanisms for maintaining QoS markings and policies across sites. Careful coordination of classification, marking, and queuing policies is necessary to avoid performance degradation when traffic crosses domain boundaries. This includes ensuring that intermediate service providers honor QoS tags and that the policies on both ends of the connection align in terms of class definitions and bandwidth guarantees.

Monitoring and visibility are critical for maintaining effective QoS in data centers. Tools such as flow analyzers, packet capture appliances, and switch telemetry provide insights into traffic patterns, queue utilization, latency, and drop rates. These metrics allow administrators to identify congestion points, validate QoS configurations, and optimize resource allocation. In modern environments, telemetry is often streamed to centralized analytics platforms that apply machine learning to detect anomalies, predict future congestion, and recommend policy adjustments. This real-time feedback loop enhances the agility and responsiveness of data center QoS management.

As data centers continue to evolve with trends such as edge computing, hybrid cloud, and artificial intelligence workloads, the role of QoS becomes even more essential. Applications are becoming more distributed, data flows more dynamic, and performance expectations more stringent. A robust QoS strategy in the data center ensures that critical services remain responsive, resource contention is managed intelligently, and the overall infrastructure operates efficiently and predictably. QoS is no longer an optional enhancement but a fundamental requirement for achieving the high availability, scalability, and performance demanded by today's digital enterprises.

Chapter 48: Future Trends in QoS Technologies

As networks continue to evolve in complexity, scale, and function, Quality of Service technologies are also transforming to meet new performance demands across highly dynamic, application-driven environments. The future of QoS is being shaped by emerging technologies such as artificial intelligence, machine learning, intent-based networking, network function virtualization, 5G, edge computing, and next-generation transport protocols. These advancements are not merely enhancements of existing QoS techniques but represent a redefinition of how service quality is measured, enforced, and optimized in real time. The focus is shifting from static, device-centric configurations to agile, intelligent, and automated approaches that can adapt to rapidly changing conditions and workloads.

One of the most significant trends in the future of QoS is the integration of artificial intelligence and machine learning into network operations. Traditional QoS requires administrators to manually configure traffic classes, assign bandwidth allocations, and monitor performance. However, AI-driven QoS systems are capable of learning from traffic behavior, user interactions, and network conditions to predict congestion, identify anomalies, and dynamically adjust policies. These systems leverage vast amounts of telemetry data, collected in real time, to make fine-grained decisions that optimize network performance without human intervention. For example, a machine learning algorithm could detect an emerging video conferencing session and automatically prioritize it by adjusting queue weights or reallocating bandwidth based on historical performance data and application sensitivity.

Another major development is the move toward intent-based networking, where administrators define desired outcomes rather than low-level configurations. In this model, QoS policies are expressed in terms of business goals, such as ensuring high reliability for voice communications or maintaining minimal latency for transaction systems. The network infrastructure then interprets these intents and automatically applies the appropriate QoS policies across the relevant devices and paths. This abstraction simplifies QoS deployment, reduces configuration errors, and allows for more agile adaptation to changes in application behavior or user demands. Intent-based QoS is especially powerful in large-scale environments, such as multi-cloud or hybrid architectures, where maintaining consistent policies manually is impractical.

Network Function Virtualization and software-defined networking are also reshaping how QoS is applied across networks. With NFV, traditional hardware-based network functions such as routers, firewalls, and load balancers are implemented in software and deployed on commodity hardware. This enables greater flexibility in how QoS is applied because network functions can be instantiated and modified on demand. SDN, by separating the control plane from the data plane, allows centralized controllers to define and push QoS policies dynamically based on real-time metrics. Together, NFV and SDN provide a platform for programmable QoS that can respond to changing network conditions, application workloads, or user profiles in an automated and scalable manner.

The emergence of 5G networks is another key driver of new QoS technologies. Unlike previous generations of mobile networks, 5G is designed to support ultra-reliable low-latency communications, massive machine-type communications, and enhanced mobile broadband on the same infrastructure. This diversity of use cases demands a more sophisticated QoS model that can isolate traffic types, enforce strict performance guarantees, and dynamically allocate network slices with dedicated resources. 5G introduces the concept of network slicing, where virtualized end-to-end networks are created for specific applications or customers, each with its own QoS profile. This allows service providers to deliver differentiated services for applications such as autonomous vehicles, industrial automation, and immersive gaming while maintaining isolation and performance consistency.

Edge computing is another trend that influences the future of QoS. As data processing moves closer to the edge to reduce latency and bandwidth consumption, QoS policies must be extended to edge nodes, gateways, and micro data centers. This decentralization requires new models of policy distribution, enforcement, and monitoring. Traditional centralized QoS mechanisms are often insufficient in edge environments, where decisions must be made locally and instantly. Edge-aware QoS frameworks will be needed to support time-sensitive applications such as augmented reality, predictive maintenance, and smart grid control systems. These frameworks must balance global policy coherence with local optimization, ensuring that edge resources are utilized efficiently while maintaining end-to-end service quality.

Another emerging aspect is the evolution of transport protocols designed with QoS in mind. Protocols like QUIC, developed by Google and now adopted as a standard by the IETF, incorporate features such as multiplexed streams, connection migration, and built-in encryption. These capabilities enhance performance and resilience in modern network environments but also require new methods of QoS enforcement that can operate effectively over encrypted and multiplexed flows. Traditional packet inspection is no longer feasible in many cases, so future QoS systems must rely more heavily on metadata, flow behavior, and endpoint signaling to determine how traffic should be classified and prioritized. This will lead to greater collaboration between application developers and network engineers to define QoS signaling mechanisms that are both secure and effective.

Cloud-native networking is also transforming how QoS is delivered. As applications become containerized and orchestrated by platforms like Kubernetes, QoS must be enforced at the pod and service mesh levels. Kubernetes already supports resource requests and limits for CPU and memory, and similar capabilities are being extended to network resources. Service meshes such as Istio or Linkerd introduce proxies that can observe and manage traffic between services, providing a point of enforcement for QoS policies. These proxies can prioritize traffic based on service identity, traffic patterns, or custom annotations, enabling granular and programmable QoS in cloud-native architectures. The shift toward microservices and API-driven applications increases the need for fine-grained QoS policies that can be enforced dynamically and consistently across distributed components.

Telemetry and observability will also play a pivotal role in the future of QoS technologies. Modern networks generate vast volumes of telemetry data, including metrics, logs, traces, and event streams. Analyzing this data in real time allows QoS systems to identify bottlenecks, enforce thresholds, and anticipate performance degradation before it impacts users. Streaming telemetry protocols such as gNMI and OpenConfig, combined with real-time analytics platforms, provide a foundation for closed-loop QoS automation. These systems can detect deviations from policy, assess root causes, and apply corrective actions automatically, creating self-healing networks that maintain service quality with minimal human intervention.

As digital transformation accelerates and networks continue to evolve toward greater decentralization, virtualization, and automation, QoS must also evolve to keep pace. The future of QoS technologies lies in their ability to operate across diverse infrastructures, to adapt intelligently to changing conditions, and to align closely with the needs of applications and users. Through the integration of AI, SDN, NFV, cloud-native principles, edge computing, and next-generation protocols, QoS will become more dynamic, granular, and policy-driven. These advancements will enable networks to deliver consistent and reliable performance in an increasingly complex and interconnected digital landscape.

Chapter 49: QoS Standards and Protocols Overview

Quality of Service in networking is governed by a wide array of standards and protocols developed over decades to address the need for differentiated service levels in IP-based networks. As the volume and diversity of network traffic grew—encompassing voice, video, data, and control plane communications—it became evident that best-effort delivery was insufficient for maintaining application performance and user satisfaction. To ensure that critical traffic receives preferential treatment, several international standards bodies and industry alliances established frameworks, specifications, and protocols to support QoS implementation across vendor platforms and network architectures. The most influential among these include the

Internet Engineering Task Force, the Institute of Electrical and Electronics Engineers, the International Telecommunication Union, and numerous vendor-specific innovations that have shaped QoS as it is known today.

At the core of modern IP QoS is the Differentiated Services architecture, standardized by the IETF in RFC 2474 and related documents. DiffServ replaced the earlier Integrated Services model by offering a scalable approach to QoS through packet marking rather than per-flow state maintenance. DiffServ defines the use of the DS field in the IP header to encode Differentiated Services Code Point values, which signal the desired treatment of each packet within a network. These markings do not guarantee service levels by themselves but serve as indicators for network devices to apply specific forwarding behaviors, such as queuing, shaping, or policing. DSCP values are grouped into behavior aggregates, each corresponding to a per-hop behavior, such as Expedited Forwarding for low-latency traffic or Assured Forwarding for applications requiring reliability without strict timing.

Complementing the DSCP marking scheme are protocols and mechanisms for classification, queuing, and scheduling. The IEEE 802.1p standard defines a method for Layer 2 QoS marking in Ethernet frames using the Priority Code Point field within the VLAN tag header. This standard allows switches to differentiate traffic based on eight priority levels, ranging from background to voice. These markings guide Layer 2 switches in placing traffic into appropriate hardware queues, which are then processed using mechanisms such as weighted round robin, strict priority, or deficit round robin. IEEE 802.1Q defines VLAN tagging and supports the implementation of 802.1p for prioritizing traffic within virtual LANs.

For real-time applications, especially in WAN or circuit-based networks, the ITU has defined several QoS standards under the umbrella of Y-series recommendations. These include guidelines on QoS classes, measurement methodologies, and performance objectives for different service types, such as voice, video, and data. The ITU's Y.1541 recommendation, for instance, specifies network performance parameters for IP-based services, including acceptable thresholds for delay, jitter, and packet loss. These standards provide a baseline for designing and evaluating QoS implementations in global networks, particularly where services cross administrative domains.

Another important protocol in the QoS landscape is Resource Reservation Protocol, or RSVP, defined by the IETF in RFC 2205. RSVP was a key component of the Integrated Services model and enables end systems to request specific QoS parameters from the network for each flow. RSVP establishes soft-state reservations along the path of the flow, allowing routers to allocate resources accordingly. Although RSVP is not widely deployed in modern networks due to its complexity and scalability limitations, it remains relevant in specialized scenarios such as MPLS traffic engineering and certain multicast applications. RSVP-TE, an extension for traffic engineering, is used in conjunction with MPLS to reserve paths with specific characteristics, supporting the implementation of deterministic QoS in backbone networks.

MPLS itself plays a crucial role in QoS, particularly in service provider environments. MPLS allows packets to be forwarded based on labels rather than IP headers, enabling fast and predictable path selection. The MPLS header includes a three-bit Experimental field, often used for QoS marking. These EXP bits can carry class-of-service information that determines how routers queue and forward labeled packets. MPLS supports class-based queuing and policing, making it suitable for offering differentiated services such as voice VPNs, premium internet access, or latency-sensitive enterprise applications. MPLS's ability to separate forwarding from routing enhances the ability to deliver strict QoS guarantees, especially when used with traffic engineering mechanisms.

Traffic shaping and policing rely on well-defined algorithms such as token bucket and leaky bucket, which are embedded into standards and widely adopted in networking equipment. These algorithms control the rate of traffic entering or leaving a device, ensuring compliance with traffic contracts and preventing excessive bandwidth consumption. Shaping smooths bursts by delaying packets, while policing enforces hard limits by dropping or remarking traffic that exceeds defined thresholds. These mechanisms are essential for maintaining fairness, avoiding congestion, and ensuring that high-priority traffic retains its performance advantage even in constrained environments.

QoS policies often require coordination across multiple technologies and layers. Protocols such as 802.11e extend QoS support to wireless LANs, defining enhanced distributed channel access methods to prioritize voice, video, best-effort, and background traffic. This standard allows wireless access points and clients to compete for airtime based on traffic class, providing better support for latency-sensitive applications in mobile environments. In LTE and 5G, QoS is implemented through bearer management and quality class indicators, ensuring that user traffic receives appropriate treatment over the radio and core network. These mobile QoS frameworks define parameters such as guaranteed bit rate, delay budget, and priority level, which are enforced across network elements from the device to the internet gateway.

Emerging protocols and frameworks continue to redefine the QoS landscape. Segment Routing, for instance, allows source nodes to define explicit paths through the network by encoding a sequence of segments in the packet header. This enables precise traffic engineering and policy enforcement without maintaining per-flow state in intermediate routers. Segment Routing integrates with QoS by associating specific segments with traffic classes or service levels, enabling more granular control over path selection and resource usage. Similarly, application-layer protocols such as HTTP/3 and QUIC introduce challenges and opportunities for QoS enforcement, as they operate over encrypted transport layers and multiplex traffic across single connections, requiring new approaches to traffic identification and prioritization.

Standardization efforts are also focusing on QoS interoperability in multi-vendor, multi-domain environments. Initiatives like MEF's Lifecycle Service Orchestration define service attributes and performance objectives for carrier Ethernet and hybrid services, allowing customers to specify QoS requirements and receive verifiable performance guarantees. These standards facilitate automation, SLA assurance, and dynamic service provisioning across interconnected networks. They also promote alignment between business objectives and technical QoS implementations, closing the gap between network configuration and service delivery.

The overview of QoS standards and protocols reveals a multi-layered and evolving landscape, where legacy mechanisms coexist with innovative architectures. While the fundamental goals remain the same—ensuring predictable and efficient delivery of network traffic—new technologies and applications continuously redefine how these goals are achieved. Understanding the standards and protocols that underpin QoS is essential for designing networks that meet modern performance demands while remaining scalable, interoperable, and adaptable to future requirements. These standards provide the foundation upon which QoS strategies are built and offer the guidance needed to ensure consistent service levels across increasingly diverse and complex network environments.

Chapter 50: Regulatory and Compliance Aspects

Quality of Service in network environments is not only a matter of performance optimization but also a subject increasingly scrutinized by regulatory bodies and governed by compliance requirements. As digital infrastructure becomes more central to the functioning of modern economies, public services, and critical industries, regulators have taken a greater interest in how networks prioritize traffic, enforce service-level agreements, and ensure equitable treatment of data. From the perspective of compliance, QoS intersects with principles of net neutrality, consumer protection, data privacy, operational transparency, and service availability. Network operators and service providers must navigate a complex landscape of legal frameworks, regional policies, and industry-specific standards to ensure that their QoS practices do not violate laws or compromise accountability.

One of the most widely discussed regulatory considerations regarding QoS is the principle of net neutrality. At its core, net neutrality refers to the idea that internet service providers should treat all data on the network equally, without discriminating or charging differently by user, content, website, or application. In this context, QoS policies that prioritize certain traffic types, such as video streaming or voice over IP, can be controversial. While prioritization may be necessary to ensure quality for latency-sensitive applications, regulators may view such practices as preferential treatment that could stifle competition or limit user choice. Different countries have adopted varying stances on net neutrality, with some allowing reasonable network management practices that include QoS for technical reasons, while others impose strict prohibitions on any form of traffic prioritization.

In the United States, for instance, the Federal Communications Commission has taken different positions on net neutrality over time, depending on the prevailing political and regulatory climate. Service providers operating in this environment must therefore monitor ongoing changes and be prepared to adapt their QoS policies accordingly. In the European Union, Regulation (EU) 2015/2120 establishes rules to safeguard open internet access, requiring ISPs to treat all traffic equally, subject to exceptions for reasonable traffic management. This regulation permits QoS differentiation only if it is necessary to comply with legal obligations, preserve network integrity, or mitigate congestion, and such measures must be proportionate and transparent. As a result, European network operators must clearly document their QoS mechanisms and demonstrate that they are not being used to unfairly favor specific content or services.

Transparency is a major theme in QoS-related regulation. Many regulatory frameworks require network operators to disclose their traffic management practices to both regulators and end-users. This includes publishing information about how different types of traffic are prioritized, what performance metrics are guaranteed, and how service degradation is handled during periods of congestion. Such disclosures are intended to help consumers make informed decisions and to hold providers accountable for the services they advertise. QoS policies that lack transparency or result in inconsistent performance can lead to regulatory fines, customer complaints, and reputational damage. Ensuring that QoS configurations are well-documented, auditable, and aligned with published service commitments is a critical component of compliance.

QoS also plays a significant role in compliance with service-level agreements, particularly in enterprise and carrier-grade networks. Organizations that offer managed services or cloud-based applications often enter into SLAs that specify minimum thresholds for latency, jitter, packet loss, and availability. These contracts are legally binding and subject to penalties if performance falls below agreed-upon levels. To comply with SLAs, service providers must implement robust QoS frameworks capable of enforcing traffic priorities and allocating resources in a way that guarantees performance for mission-critical applications. Regular monitoring, reporting, and verification of QoS metrics are necessary to demonstrate SLA compliance and to support dispute resolution in cases of service disruption or degradation.

In regulated industries such as finance, healthcare, energy, and government, QoS compliance extends beyond performance metrics to include requirements for reliability, availability, and redundancy. Financial trading platforms, for example, must meet strict latency requirements to ensure fair market access and to prevent information asymmetry. Healthcare networks must support real-time telemedicine and remote monitoring with guaranteed bandwidth and low delay, as required by medical device regulations and patient safety standards. In such sectors, failure to deliver consistent QoS can have legal, financial, or even life-threatening consequences. Regulatory bodies in these industries may require certifications, periodic audits, and conformance to specific technical standards as part of their oversight activities.

Data protection laws such as the General Data Protection Regulation in Europe also intersect with QoS in important ways. While QoS policies primarily concern traffic performance, the methods used for classification and prioritization can involve inspecting packet headers or payloads. If these inspections reveal personal data or user identifiers, they may fall under the scope of data protection regulations. This means that QoS implementations must respect privacy principles, avoid excessive data collection, and ensure that any personal information processed for traffic management purposes is protected by appropriate security controls. In some cases, organizations may be required to conduct data protection impact assessments to evaluate the risks of their QoS policies and to implement safeguards accordingly.

Regulatory compliance in the context of QoS also involves the use of lawful interception and data retention practices. Law enforcement agencies may require access to certain types of traffic or metadata for investigative purposes, and network operators must be able to provide this access without compromising QoS. At the same time, they must ensure that lawful interception capabilities do not introduce latency, packet loss, or instability for affected traffic flows. Balancing the demands of regulatory compliance with the technical requirements of QoS is a delicate task that necessitates careful design and rigorous testing of network systems.

Standards organizations also contribute to QoS compliance by publishing frameworks and best practices that align with regulatory expectations. The International Organization for Standardization, for instance, has published ISO/IEC 20000 for IT service management, which includes requirements for service performance and monitoring. Similarly, the Metro Ethernet Forum and the ITU have defined performance objectives and testing methodologies that can be used to demonstrate compliance with national and international regulations. By adhering to these standards, organizations can reduce the risk of regulatory non-compliance and improve their overall service quality posture.

The rise of cloud computing and global connectivity adds further complexity to regulatory compliance in QoS. Data and applications may traverse multiple jurisdictions, each with its own regulatory requirements. Providers must ensure that QoS policies are consistent across these domains and that service guarantees are not compromised by cross-border latency, inconsistent enforcement, or inadequate visibility. Multi-national enterprises must work closely with legal, compliance, and network operations teams to map out their obligations and ensure that QoS implementations are both technically effective and legally sound.

In the broader context of digital rights and ethical networking, QoS compliance may also involve considerations related to accessibility, inclusion, and fair access. Network prioritization should not disadvantage vulnerable populations, nor should it create barriers to information or essential services. Regulators and advocacy groups increasingly evaluate QoS policies not only on technical grounds but also through the lens of social impact, pushing for equitable design principles and inclusive connectivity strategies.

Ensuring compliance in QoS is not a one-time activity but an ongoing process that requires alignment between policy, engineering, legal, and operational domains. As the regulatory landscape evolves alongside technological innovation, organizations must remain vigilant, agile, and transparent in how they define and implement QoS. The ability to guarantee performance while respecting legal and ethical obligations is becoming a core competency for modern networked organizations operating in a world that is both highly connected and increasingly regulated.

Chapter 51: Case Studies in QoS Deployment

The deployment of Quality of Service across various industries and network architectures provides practical insights into how theoretical concepts are applied to solve real-world challenges. Case studies in QoS deployment offer concrete examples of how organizations implement traffic prioritization, manage congestion, and ensure performance for critical applications. These examples span diverse environments including enterprises, service providers, healthcare institutions, financial systems, and educational campuses. Each deployment reflects unique technical goals, operational constraints, and business drivers, but all share a common objective: to deliver consistent and reliable service in increasingly complex and dynamic network ecosystems.

One notable case study comes from a large multinational corporation with globally distributed offices and data centers. The company faced frequent performance issues with its voice-over-IP systems and video conferencing tools, particularly during peak business hours. Complaints of dropped calls, frozen video feeds, and poor audio quality were disrupting business operations and diminishing productivity. The IT department launched a QoS deployment initiative focused on classifying and prioritizing real-time traffic across their MPLS-based WAN and internal LAN segments. They began by performing a full traffic analysis using NetFlow and packet capture tools to identify the most bandwidth-sensitive applications. Based on this data, they developed a classification policy that placed VoIP and video traffic in a high-priority queue, transactional business applications in a medium-priority class, and best-effort for general internet browsing and email. The policies were enforced at every router and switch across their network using DSCP markings, strict-priority queuing, and traffic shaping at WAN edges. Within two months of deploying the new QoS policies, the organization saw a significant drop in complaints and measurable improvements in call quality and video performance across all sites.

In another example, a major healthcare provider needed to deploy QoS to support a wide range of digital health services, including telemedicine, medical imaging transfers, and electronic health records. The network team faced the challenge of ensuring that mission-critical applications received appropriate bandwidth while keeping patient data secure and maintaining compliance with HIPAA regulations. To achieve this, the team segmented the network by application type, using VLANs and access control lists to isolate traffic between departments. They then implemented class-based QoS using Cisco devices to assign bandwidth guarantees and latency thresholds for imaging systems and voice traffic used in telehealth consultations. Packet marking and queuing policies were carefully designed to reflect clinical urgency, with real-time monitoring dashboards that alerted administrators to any deviations from expected performance. The QoS deployment enabled radiologists to receive scans in near real time and allowed doctors to conduct virtual consultations without interruptions, directly improving patient care while maintaining full visibility and compliance over network usage.

A large university campus offers another illustrative example of effective QoS deployment. The institution had been experiencing poor wireless performance during lectures, where hundreds of students would simultaneously connect to the network to stream video, participate in live polling, or download course materials. The situation worsened during major campus events when guest devices further saturated the network. The IT department implemented a tiered QoS strategy on both wired and wireless infrastructure. Wi-Fi access points were configured with WMM QoS to prioritize voice and video traffic. The wireless controllers and core switches were upgraded to support deep packet inspection and application-aware traffic shaping. Educational applications and learning management systems were given higher priority, while entertainment services like video streaming and gaming were throttled during academic hours. The QoS policies were dynamically applied based on the time of day and user role, with professors and administrators receiving higher network privileges. After the deployment, students experienced smoother video playback during lectures, and network congestion was significantly reduced without requiring additional bandwidth investments.

In the financial sector, a leading investment bank deployed QoS to support its high-frequency trading infrastructure. The bank operated data centers in multiple global locations with millisecond-level synchronization requirements. Even the slightest delay in data transmission could lead to substantial financial losses. The network was designed with deterministic QoS in mind, using MPLS circuits with guaranteed latency SLAs and QoS markings tightly controlled from end to end. RSVP was used for bandwidth reservation, and priority queuing ensured that trading orders and market data were always placed ahead of other less sensitive traffic. The data center switches supported hardware timestamping and microburst mitigation, allowing for ultra-low-latency traffic flows. The QoS implementation extended to the desktop trading terminals, which were placed on dedicated VLANs with strict network access policies and traffic shaping. The result was a highly predictable and resilient trading environment that supported the bank's operational goals with full regulatory compliance and technical rigor.

Service providers also offer compelling examples of QoS deployment at scale. A regional internet service provider in Latin America introduced tiered QoS services for small and medium-sized business customers. Customers could choose from different service levels, each offering different guarantees for voice, video, and general web traffic. The provider used policy-based routing and traffic policing at the edge routers to enforce service-level agreements. Real-time dashboards allowed customers to monitor their usage and performance metrics. By offering QoS as a premium service, the provider differentiated itself in a competitive market and reduced churn among its business clientele. This approach not only improved customer satisfaction but also enabled better capacity planning and traffic engineering across the backbone network.

Another innovative deployment occurred in a smart city initiative where QoS was essential to support connected traffic lights, public safety communications, and surveillance systems. City planners and network engineers worked together to establish a municipal fiber network that prioritized emergency services and sensor data over public Wi-Fi and administrative traffic. QoS policies were implemented using SDN controllers that dynamically reconfigured the network based on real-time events. During emergencies, such as a fire or public gathering, the system could instantly elevate the priority of communication channels used by first responders, ensuring low-latency and high-reliability connectivity. The smart city platform benefited from high availability, situational responsiveness, and scalable QoS enforcement that supported multiple agencies and use cases without infrastructure duplication.

These case studies illustrate how QoS is not a one-size-fits-all solution but rather a set of principles and mechanisms that must be tailored to the specific requirements of the network and its users. Whether the goal is to ensure reliable communication for remote healthcare, to preserve low-latency paths for financial trading, or to deliver seamless user experiences on a university campus, QoS deployments require a clear understanding of traffic patterns, application priorities, and operational constraints. By aligning technical implementation with business objectives, organizations across sectors are leveraging QoS to build networks that are not only faster but also smarter, more efficient, and more responsive to the needs of their users.

Chapter 52: Final Thoughts and Best Practices

Implementing Quality of Service in modern networks is both an art and a science. It requires a deep understanding of network behavior, traffic patterns, and application requirements, as well as a practical approach to engineering solutions that adapt to complexity and change. QoS is no longer an optional feature reserved for high-end service providers or specialized enterprise use cases. It has become an essential component in almost every network where performance, reliability, and predictability are critical. From voice and video applications to cloud services, IoT, and real-time analytics, the demand for efficient traffic management is rising, and QoS offers the tools to meet these evolving expectations.

One of the most important best practices in QoS deployment is to begin with comprehensive network assessment and traffic analysis. Before applying any policies or enabling prioritization mechanisms, it is essential to understand what kinds of traffic are present in the network, which applications are most critical, and how resources are being consumed. Tools such as flow analysis, deep packet inspection, and packet captures provide valuable insights into where bottlenecks exist, which applications are most sensitive to delay or jitter, and which endpoints generate or consume the most bandwidth. This data forms the foundation for intelligent classification policies that accurately reflect business priorities.

Accurate classification is the cornerstone of effective QoS. Without it, packets cannot be properly marked, queued, or shaped. Classification should be as granular as needed but as simple as possible to manage. Ideally, traffic should be classified based on a combination of protocol, port, IP address range, application signature, or even user identity if supported by the network. Traffic should be divided into a small number of classes—typically voice, video, mission-critical data, best-effort, and background—each with its own treatment model. Overcomplicating the classification schema can make troubleshooting difficult and reduce the efficiency of queuing and scheduling mechanisms.

Once classification is in place, consistent marking must follow. Marking should occur as close to the edge of the network as possible, ideally on the originating device or access switch. Markings such as DSCP or IEEE 802.1p values should be preserved throughout the network to ensure that traffic is handled consistently across hops. Trust boundaries must be defined clearly. For example, edge devices that cannot be trusted to mark traffic correctly should have their markings overridden by upstream policy. This prevents abuse and ensures that high-priority treatment is reserved for authorized and valid traffic types.

Queuing strategies must match the operational environment. For low-latency applications such as VoIP and video conferencing, strict-priority queues are often required, but they should be policed to avoid starvation of other queues. For other traffic types, weighted fair queuing or class-based weighted fair queuing ensures that each class receives its allocated share of bandwidth. Queue tuning, including buffer sizes and drop thresholds, should be guided by empirical performance data. In high-speed data centers or core networks, hardware-assisted queuing is often preferred to minimize overhead and support high throughput with minimal latency.

Traffic shaping and policing are two powerful tools that should be applied judiciously. Shaping smooths traffic bursts and prevents congestion on slower links, making it useful on WAN interfaces or outbound internet connections. Policing, while more aggressive, can enforce strict limits and prevent abusive flows from consuming more than their fair share of bandwidth. Each has its role, and the choice depends on the nature of the traffic and the operational objectives. Policing may be used at the edge for non-critical applications, while shaping may be reserved for critical traffic that should not be dropped indiscriminately.

Monitoring and verification must be part of the QoS lifecycle. QoS is not a one-time configuration exercise but an ongoing process that requires validation and refinement. Tools such as SNMP, NetFlow, telemetry, and packet capture provide the visibility needed to confirm that policies are functioning as intended. Performance dashboards should display real-time metrics such as queue depth, drop rates, latency, and jitter per class of service. Alerts should be configured for anomalies or threshold breaches, enabling network engineers to take proactive corrective action before end-user experience is affected.

Documentation is another often-overlooked aspect of QoS deployment. Every QoS policy, class map, queue configuration, and interface assignment should be well-documented. This is not only helpful for ongoing maintenance and troubleshooting but also essential for regulatory compliance, SLA management, and knowledge transfer between teams. Standardized naming conventions for class maps and policies can help reduce confusion and improve readability in large environments.

Training and awareness are crucial for long-term QoS success. Network teams must understand the rationale behind each policy and how QoS mechanisms function on different platforms and devices. Operations staff should be equipped to interpret QoS metrics and respond to alerts. Change control processes should include QoS validation to ensure that new services or configurations do not unintentionally disrupt established prioritization schemes.

Cross-team collaboration is also a best practice. QoS is not solely a network function; it intersects with application performance, security, compliance, and user experience. Working with application owners, system administrators, and security teams ensures that QoS policies are aligned with business needs and operational realities. For example, understanding how an application handles retransmissions or adapts to latency can inform more effective traffic treatment. Security teams can ensure that traffic marking does not introduce vulnerabilities or compromise data confidentiality.

Scalability and future-proofing should be considered early in the design. QoS policies that work well in a small environment may not scale to global networks with thousands of endpoints. Hierarchical QoS, SD-WAN, and cloud-native networking principles should be incorporated to support growth and maintain consistency across hybrid architectures. Automated policy deployment through templates, orchestration tools, and infrastructure-as-code approaches can reduce manual errors and accelerate rollout.

Ultimately, QoS is a discipline of control. It allows network administrators to move beyond reactive troubleshooting and into proactive service assurance. It empowers organizations to prioritize what matters most, to prevent disruption, and to support strategic initiatives such as digital transformation, cloud migration, and real-time collaboration. When designed thoughtfully, implemented with precision, and monitored continuously, QoS becomes an invisible enabler of user satisfaction and business continuity.

The lessons learned across industries and the best practices outlined through years of evolution make one point clear: QoS is not about restricting traffic, but about enabling performance. It brings structure to network unpredictability and ensures that every packet, flow, and application receives the treatment it deserves based on its importance. As networks grow more dynamic and interconnected, QoS will remain a foundational element in delivering efficient, secure, and high-performing services across every layer of the digital enterprise.

www.ingramcontent.com/pod-product-compliance
Lightning Source LLC
La Vergne TN
LVHW051234050326
832903LV00028B/2403